GRE® PREP

2020-2021

by

GARY HILL

Published by

Cambridge Test Prep Publishing

D1361781

Contents

About this book 1

How to use this book 2

Exam Secrets! 3

How should i prepare for tests and exams? 4

Some general (but important) information about the GRE ® general test 7

General Advice 10

Verbal reasoning 14

GRE Quantitative Reasoning 26

Analytical Writing 55

Section 1: Issue topic 106

Section 2: Argument topic 107

Section 3: Quantitative reasoning 109

Section 4 Verbal reasoning 117

Section 5: Quantitative reasoning 130

Section 6: Verbal reasoning 139

Answers 147

About this book

This book is a no-nonsense guide to acing your GRE. I will teach you about the different question types, how to study, how to prepare on the day, how ace the exam and get into the school of your dreams. A lot of books have excess detail and boring content, but not this one! I have cut the fluff and made a fast-paced guide ready to help you get the most out of every second. I have included all the key details you need to give you the key ingredients to acing your GRE.

I will not only teach you how to master each question type, but I will also show you how to maximize your efforts; both in studying, and in the exam room! So many students have the knowledge but underperform on the day, with my hints and tips you will get every point available to.

It is best used as a study guide, read it, get the information that you need, and then study each section of questions independently. Use my useful hints and tips on effective studying (proven by research) and then, when you're ready, attempt the practice tests.

I wish you the best of luck in your studies, and hope that this book gets you in to the school that you desire!

How to use this book

You can't underestimate the importance of doing well in the high-pressure high-stakes environment of test day. How well you do on the GRE will have a significant impact on your future- and I have the research and practical advice to help you execute on test day.

The book you're reading now is designed to help you avoid the most common errors test-takers frequently make.

I don't want to waste your time. My study guide is fast-paced and fluff-free. I suggest going through it a number of times, as repetition is an important part of learning new information and concepts.

First, read through the study guide completely to get a feel for the content and organization. Read the general success strategies first, and then proceed to the content sections. Each tip has been carefully selected for its effectiveness.

Second, read through the study guide again, and take notes in the margins and highlight those sections where you may have a particular weakness.

Finally, bring the Study guide with you on test day and have one last run through before the exam begins.

Exam Secrets!

This section is all about how best to prepare for any exam, before and after, it's worth reading: get all the detail you need about preparing and how to act in an exam!

With any and all exams it is absolutely crucial that you prepare properly and that you have all the hints and tricks that you can have, available to you. The whole point of this book is to help you to not only learn about the GRE, about each question type and to practice the exams but also to help you get every extra mark that you can.

No time to hang about; let's look at how best to prepare for test and exams.

How should I prepare for tests and exams?

I spoke to the experts and have all the details on how to prepare for exams (of any kind). You should treat the GRE like any other normal exam, how your teachers wanted you to prepare in high school! Prepare effectively in the build-up to it and you will get the score that you need. If you follow this advice you give yourself the best chance of Acing your GRE, and any other exam for that matter so, as I teach you all about the rest of the exam, make sure you follow the good study habits all the way!

Without further ado, please check out my advice below.

Good Study Habits - what to do in the build-up to the exams.

1. Don't cram at the last second;, try studying for 60-90 minutes per day for a week leading up to an exam. All-nighters simply don't work for most people, and students experience declining returns on their efforts when they attempt to study for four and five hours straight.

2. If you have any outstanding questions, get help at least three days before the exam. You'll be able to go to office hours with an agenda if you've given yourself a mock test in advance.

3. Think about what written questions on the exam might be; outline every potential essay as a form of pre-testing and practice.

4. Use the elimination process on multiple-choice, matching questions. You may also want to cover the options first for multiple choice questions, and try answering the question on your own. Thus you will find the options for the answer less confusing. Make sure that you are aware of context, relationships and positionality between concepts, and multiple definitions of terms, as you prepare for multiple choice

exams. A deep understanding of the vocabulary is a key to multiple-choice exam success.

5. Keep up with your work. keep up with readings, and take notes conscientiously, studying can be a relatively pain-free process. Make sure to review and expand upon notes regularly throughout the. Consider developing a glossary or collection of note cards for vocabulary review . Many students find that preparing for an individual class for 60-90 minutes per day, five or six days per week, will leave them well-prepared at exam time.

6. Find a group of other committed students to train with. A group study session is an ideal time for reviewing and comparing notes, asking each other questions, explaining ideas to each other, discussing the upcoming examination and difficult concepts, and delegating study tasks where appropriate. Set your group study session with an agenda and a specific timeframe, so that your work together is not off-topic.

7. Make sure you get lots of sleep. The time spent asleep is often the time when we synthesize information completely, especially the topics that are covered in the few hours before bedtime. Once you take the test you want to be as new as possible to be able to fully engage your working memory.

8. Find ways to apply materials. Think about how course topics relate to your personal interests, societal issues and controversies, issues that have been raised in other classes, or different life experiences.

9. Develop a good routine 'morning-of' Eat a good breakfast. Go ahead and play something upbeat if the music gets you going. Get some physical exercise, even if it's a brief walk or stretch. If you feel nervous, record your anxieties on paper or use mental imagery to imagine doing something you enjoy and then apply those feelings to the exam. Think of preparing to a performance like an athlete before a contest or a musician.

10. Create an assault plan. Write down the key terms or formulas you need before you continue. Think how you are going to use the allotted time.

11. If you have time at the end of the exam, go back and reread your work and look again at multiple-choice questions. Check to see that you answered every question before you take the exam. But remember, your first answer is usually the best one. Be extremely careful about changing the answers later on.

12. Do not do lots of different things while studying. Set time to study beforehand and follow through. This means leaving your dormitory room for most people and turning off visual/auditory distractions, including iPods, Facebook, and lyric music.

13. Reward yourself, please. If you've been studying conscientiously for a week or more, you should take a little time to relax before you start your studies again.

14. Carefully read out the directions.

15. Write a brief outline of the essay questions before beginning.

16. Leave to the end the most time-consuming problems, especially the ones with low point values.

17. Concentrate on the matter at hand. If you do the test one step at a time, you will find it far less likely to be overwhelming.

18. If you're stuck on a question, bypass that question. Mark the question off so at the end of the exam you can get back to it.

19. Take a moment to review your test preparation strategy. Take into account what has worked and what needs to be improved. In particular, take a moment to see if your study group was helpful. If you feel that your test-preparation strategies need changing, do so!

20. Complete a mock test. Why not set aside an hour, and try to answer questions on a paper without using your notes? If you complete a mock test 3-4 days before an exam, you'll then know where to focus your studying. You may also combat pre-test jitters by demonstrating to yourself what you know. Try answering a couple of potential essay questions on a timed, closed book basis and see how you do. Another simple way to conduct a mock test is to ask a friend or classmate to give you an oral quiz based on concepts in the textbook or in either of your notes.

Some general (but important) information about the GRE ® general test

The GRE provides schools with an excellent assessment of the skills you need to succeed in MBA and specialized master's degree programs. It is viewed on par with other graduate admissions tests by the world's top business schools.

Business schools that are the best in the world use the GRE alongside other graduate admissions tests to provide them with an assessment of the skills needed to succeed at MBA or other Masters qualifications.

The test contains 3 sections: Analytical Writing, Verbal Reasoning and Quantitative Reasoning. GRE® scores are accepted at graduate and business schools.

Only the GRE can be used to apply to both business and graduate schools but it's always worth checking that your intended school will accept it.

Your Score is valid for five years this means you can take it now and have plenty of time to think about your options.

You don't have to send in your scores; with the ScoreSelect ® option if you think you haven't done your best. You have the opportunity to check your result and then only submit the best set of scores to your dream school.

Test Content and Structure

The GRE comes in six parts, known as sections. The first part will always be the analytical writing segment with individually constructed query and argument questions. The next five divisions include two segments of verbal reasoning, two pieces of quantitative reasoning, and either experimental or research section. These five parts can occur in any order. The experimental portion does not count towards your final score but is not separated in the exam, so you don't which section it is! The whole exam takes about 3 hours 45 mins in total.

Of these sections, the Analytical writing is broken into two parts, one portion for each issue and the argument section. The next four parts compose of two verbal and two quantitative sections in different orders. There is no experimental section of the paper-based study but you will only sit the paper version in an area where there is no access to the computer testing centres.

Verbal section

On the computer based test, you will still be assessed on reading comprehension, critical reasoning, and vocabulary usage. The verbal test is scored between 130–170, with scores increasing by 1 each time. In a most of your examinations, each verbal section consists of 20 questions to be completed in 30 minutes. Every verbal section consists of about 6 text completion, 4 sentence equivalence, and 10 critical reading questions. Since 2011 there were some changes that mean that there is now a reduced emphasis on rote vocabulary knowledge. Text completion items have been included in order to replace the old sentence completions and new reading question types allowing for the selection of multiple answers were added.

These questions will test your basic high school level mathematics and reasoning skills. The quantitative test is, like the reading comprehension, scored between 130–170, in 1-point increments. Normally, each quantitative section has 20 questions and you will have 35 minutes to complete them. Each quantitative section has around 8 quantitative comparisons, 9 problem solving items, and 3 data interpretation questions. In 2011 new questions were added where you have to key in the missing number onto the computer system

Analytical writing section

The analytical writing section consists of two different essays, an "issue task" and an "argument task". The writing section is graded on a scale of 0–6, with scores increasing by 0.5 each time. The essays are written on a computer using a word processing program specifically designed by ETS. The computer doesn't have a spell checker and is basically a very simple word processor. At least two people will grade the writing and if necessary a 3rd opinion will be sought.

Issue Task

The test taker is given 30 minutes to write an essay about a selected topic and all the topics within this pool are included in this book. The pool of questions are published by the GRE, there are loads to practice with contained within this book.

Argument Task

A statement (i.e. a set of evidence and assumptions leading to a conclusion) will be presented to the test-taker and they are required to compose an article evaluating the argument. Test takers are asked to evaluate the validity of the claim and to offer recommendations about whether to strengthen the reasoning of the argument. Tests are supposed to resolve the logical shortcomings of the claim and not to have a particular opinion on the subject. The period allotted to this essay is 30 minutes. All the topics within this pool are included in this book. The pool of questions is published by the GRE.

Experimental section

The experimental section can be verbal or quantitative, contains completely new questions and although the experimental section does not count towards your score, you don't know which section it is as it appears identical to the sections that are scored. Because test takers have no definite way of knowing which section is experimental, it is typically advised that test takers try their best and be focused on every section. Sometimes an identified research section at the end of the test is given instead of the experimental section. Please note that this is not the case on the paper based test.

2011 GRE Test Update

The computer-based study was updated in 2011 in such a manner that it no longer only adapts after each problem (the same as the GMAT) but instead now only adapts between the first and second parts of each category. It means that the first segment of both Verbal and Quantitative Reasoning will have a combination of simple and difficult questions. The complexity of your second segments can depend on how well you do in the first segments. The Software has a big pool of test questions of varying degrees of difficulty; students who do well in their first sections will "unlock" a more difficult second section and earn a correspondingly higher "scaled score after the test is finished. The paper-based exam does not switch between sections, so all sections of the exam are of equal difficulty. The score for the paper-based test will be determined using the computer-based test results as a comparison.

General Advice

To complement the exam hints and tips earlier, I have included some GRE exam specific hints and tips, below.

1. Take the Easy Part First.

Within each of the sections, each question counts equally toward your score. There will inevitably be questions you are great at and questions you don't like. What is great about the GRE is that there is no need to follow the order given in the test; each question is worth the same! To do as well as you can: leave the questions you don't think you can answer for last. If you are going to run out of time anywhere make sure that the ones that you don't answer are the ones you were unlikely to score well on anyway. If you do this, you will go through each section twice, first time around: answer the questions you like. Get all of those easy points in the bank. Leave the difficult ones until the end, that way you know how long you have for those particular questions.

2. Mark and Return

If you see a problem you don't like, a question that looks hard, or a question that looks energy-consuming, leave it and come back to it. This doesn't always work; the problem may be more complicated than it seemed, or you may have simply misread it, and it seems hard just because you're dealing with the wrong information, however it is a really useful strategy. The GRE is almost a four-hour exam. You will get tired working for four hours. When that happens, the misreading of a problem and making a mistake is almost inevitable. As soon as this happens it's difficult to unread the question and see it correctly. As long as you're still in problems, you could try it at least ten times in a row, and you'll read it the same wrong way every time. Whether a question is easier than it appeared, or rendered more difficult by the fact that you skipped a key phrase or piece of information, the solution you have chosen is not working. Leave the problem, comeback to it later. When you walk away, the brain doesn't just forget about what you've looked at, it keeps on thinking it over. The noise of the other questions allows your brain to consider the issue from some other perspectives. When you come back to the problem, you may notice that the component that has caused you so much trouble with the most recent time is now mysteriously obvious. If you're still having trouble with the problem, walk away again. If you stay with the question for too long, then you may waste all your time there. Mark it, and come back to it at the end, if you have time.

3. Use the Review Screen to Navigate

You can mark an answer or unanswered question and Come back to it later on it the exam to do so: click the "Go to Query" icon and you will return to that question directly. This opens up a whole new world of competitive possibilities for somebody who knows what they're doing (which will be you!).

4. Pace on the GRE is crucial!

The clock has a way to get the brain poisoned. The fact that a ticking timer is there causes you to make errors. The trick is to take any segment as though no clock existed. As long as you skip the hard ones, use the Mark button and return every time you have a problem, there are very few questions in a wrong section. It doesn't matter how many you answer, Precision is the important bit! Slow down, take it easy and search just with precision. Don't keep spending time when you're hitting a problem; find an easier one, and do that instead!

Be careful though! As soon as you speed up, your accuracy will decrease. There is only one exception, and that is a section's last two minutes. The same is valid for a missed question and an incorrect answer. The only change to this is at the end of a section. Quickly see which questions you have not answered, use the Review button. Please spend your time on your easiest questions. Try to collect points methodically and precisely. Go through each section twice, once with the easiest, then at the end with the hardest questions in the remaining time.

5. Get rid of the wrong answers (in multiple choices)

Since there are far more incorrect answers in the GRE than there are correct ones, you will actually be better off on some of the more difficult (which you do with your second time through) not to try get the best answers, but by spotting which options are incorrect, and removing them, then making an educated guess at the remaining answers. There are solutions to most of the problems and one of them is the right one, so delete the wrong ones, and make a guess out of what remains. Some of them are clearly wrong and can be eliminated as a result. Sometimes in fact it can be easier to identify and eliminate wrong answers than to identify the right ones. You can do this for the questions based on vocabulary, which will contain a lot of words you don't know. You cannot identify the correct answer in relation to such questions, but you can definitely identify some incorrect ones.

Get rid of the wrong ones so you'll have a better chance when you guess. The same applies to questions about reading comprehension, which contain many obviously wrong answers. ETS loves to suck you into more maths than is really necessary on the math side of the test. Often, you can remove responses that are clearly too big or too small. Sometimes, even more important than doing the right math is to eliminate the wrong answers. These false answers are known as trap replies and are designed to appeal to you. Often the answers seem to shout out, "Select me! "Through a question you work. You will significantly improve your score by learning to recognize them. Improve your odds on each question type. If you can get rid of the wrong choice and improve your chances to one in four. Eliminate three, and you have a good chance of earning points by guessing, remember that there are no points on the test for working out; it's all about whether you get the correct answer, so delete the ones that are obviously incorrect!

6. Use Your Scratch Paper

If ETS are going to give you some scratch paper to work with, they must do it for a reason. Use every piece of additional help that you can, which includes scratch paper. You will get six sheets of scratch paper stapled into a booklet. You can get more by raising your hand during a section, but that takes time, so you will need an efficient system for using scratch paper. It's better to park your thinking on your scratch paper. Get it out of your head and onto the page. Good things happen when you do. On the math side, scratch paper is crucial. Not only is it important for performing complicated calculations, but when used properly, it can actually help to direct your thinking as you work through multi-step problems.

8. Let It Go

Whenever you start a new segment, concentrate on this chapter and leave the last segment behind you. Talk not of that frustrating synonym from the earlier part because the new question is all about geometry. You cannot get it back and, you'll always think that you've done much worse than you actually have.

9. Don't Make Any Last-Minute Lifestyle Changes

There is no great idea making big changes in your life the week leading up to the test. That's NOT a week to stop smoking, to continue to vape, to stop drinking, to start drinking, to get a new partner, to stop or leave work. Business as usual.

Verbal reasoning

The GRE's verbal reasoning section measures your ability to analyse and evaluate written material withdraw and understand information from it, analyse relationships and asses components.

They come in many different forms which I will go into detail with, later. Around half of the segment requires reading passages and answering questions on those passages. The other half requires reading, interpreting, and completing existing texts or parts of text.

You will see three types of questions: Reading Comprehension, Text Completion, and Sentence Equivalence.

Reading Comprehension Training Questions are there to see if you have the skills needed to read and comprehend the forms of writing commonly found in graduate school.

These skills include:

- knowing the meaning of individual words
- knowing the meaning of individual sentences
- understanding the meaning loner text
- understanding the difference between a text's minor and major points
- summarizing
- drawing conclusions from text
- understanding incomplete data, inferring missing information

Each Reading Comprehension question is based on a passage that can be of varying length typically of a maximum of up to about 8 paragraphs. Passages can come from all sorts of sources and on all sorts of topics.

General Guidance for Reading Comprehension Issues:

- Reading excerpts are taken from several places, and you will come across things you haven't met yet. This doesn't matter as all questions will be addressed based on the details given in the text, so you are not required to rely on external expertise. But, if you meet a really hard section, it is wise to save it to the end.

- Consult and examine the passage thoroughly before attempting questions, and pay heed to the less specific parts of the text.

- Know the difference between the texts' ideas or facts and make a note of them

- Also, notice what the text is obviously speaking about as being as one of plausible or theoretical.

- Notice any massive swings from one theory to another.

- Start defining the connection between various concepts and make a note of it.

- Look at each question only dependent on what the text has said, do not rely on your own knowledge of the content. Occasionally your own views or viewpoints can disagree with those expressed in a passage; which is when it is extremely important to take extra special care to understand the meaning of the passage. You shouldn't presume to comply with anything you find in reading passages, you may not agree with it but the questions will ask you about what the text says, not what you think.

Multiple-Choice — Select One Description: These are normal multiple-choice questions with five potential answers to pick from.

Answering: Single Option Multiple-Choice Questions Tips

- Read all the responses before making your decision it doesn't matter if you think you already know the answer, read them all – you never know when you may have been tricked or fallen into a trap!

- The right response is one that addresses the query the best completely; be cautious not to be fooled by options that are only partly correct. Always, be cautious not to take an answer merely because it's a valid argument.

- If the question is a vocabulary question regarding a word within the passage, make sure that the answer you pick accurately reflects the way the word is used in that particular sentence. Many verbs have definitions in various ways and you need to be clear that you are using the correct one.

Multiple-Choice — Pick One or More Description: these have three choices and allow you to choose all that's correct; one, two, or all three of the choices. Can with these questions, you must pick all the correct responses, and only those; there is no credit for partly correct responses.

Tips for Addressing Multiple Options Multiple-Choice Questions

- Judge each answer choice individually on its own, ignore the other choices

- A right answer option 100% correctly answers the question; be cautious not to be confused by either partly valid or partly addressing the query. Always, be cautious not to take an answer merely because it is a correct statement. This is a red herring sent to trick you!

- Don't be confused if you think all three responses are right, this is another trick, where you will need to re-read the question.

Select the sentence: The question asks you to select the sentence that meets a description.

- To answer the question, select one of the sentences.

- As discussed earlier: be sure to review each of the related sentences in the passage separately before choosing your response. Do not test any sentences in the subsections mentioned.

- The appropriate response option must fit the definition provided in the question; do not choose a statement if the is only partly appropriate, there will be options that fit these criteria, and the question is aiming to trick you.

Examples: Reading Comprehension

Now use these hints and tips to answer the below

Examples 1-3 are based on the following passage:

Reviving the practice of using elements of popular music in classical composition, an approach that had been in hibernation in the United States during the 1960s, composer Philip Glass (born 1937) embraced the ethos of popular music without imitating it. Glass based two symphonies on music by rock musicians Nigel Bowie and Brian Eno, but the symphonies' sound is distinctively his. Popular elements do not appear out of place in Glass's classical music, which from its early days has shared certain harmonies and rhythms with rock music. Yet this use of popular elements has not made Glass a composer of popular music. His music is not a version of popular music packaged to attract classical listeners; it is high art for listeners steeped in rock rather than the classics. The passage is repeated below, with the sentences numbered for convenience of reference. In the test itself, the sentences are not numbered.

1. Consider each of the three choices separately and select all that apply.

The passage suggests that Glass's work displays which of the following qualities?

(A) A return to the use of popular music in classical compositions

(B) An attempt to elevate rock music to an artistic status more closely approximating that of classical music

(C) A long-standing tendency to incorporate elements from two apparently disparate musical styles

2. The passage addresses which of the following issues related to Glass's use of popular elements in his classical compositions?

(A) How it is regarded by listeners who prefer rock to the classics

(B) How it has affected the commercial success of Glass's music

(C) Whether it has contributed to a revival of interest among other composers in using popular elements in their compositions

(D) Whether it has had a detrimental effect on Glass's reputation as a composer of classical music

(E) Whether it has caused certain of Glass's works to be derivative in quality

Select the sentence that distinguishes two ways of integrating rock and classical music.

Explanation for Reading Comprehension Questions

To answer the first question, determining each response option independently is necessary. Since the passage says Glass has revived traditional music use in classical compositions, answer choice A is obviously correct. On the other side, the passage still rejects that Glass composes popular music or bundles it to elevate its prestige, and answer choice B is incorrect. Ultimately, since Glass's style always combined rock elements with classical elements, response option C is right. Moving to the second question, one of the important points the passage makes is that when Glass incorporates popular elements in his music, the effect is his own development (it's "distinctly his"). In other words, music isn't synthetic. Therefore, one subject the passage addresses is the one referred to in response option E — it answers it in the negative. The passage does not address the effect of Glass's use of popular elements at audiences, the commercial success of his music, other composers, or Glass's credibility, so none of A through D's choices are correct. Finally, almost every passage sentence refers to integrating rock music into classical compositions, but only the last sentence distinguishes two forms. It differs between writing rock music in a way that will draw classical listeners and writing classical music that will attract listeners familiar with rock. The last sentence is the correct answer.

Text Completion

As described above, professional readers do not simply absorb the information presented on the page; rather, they maintain a constant mind-set of analysis and assessment, thinking about what they have read so far to build an overall picture and refine it as they go. Text Completion questions assess this skill by omitting key words from short passages and allowing the test taker to use the remaining passage details as a guide to choose words or short phrases to fill the blanks and construct a cohesive argument.

Text Completion Question Details

- Has one to five sentences

- One to three blanks spaces

- Answer choices for various blanks do not affect what you choose on the next blank.

- Recognise parts of the text that seem very important, either because they reinforce the context of the passage (terms like "except" or "over"), or because they are central to explaining what the passage is about.

- When reading, fill in the words in your head and then see if the solution options give similar terms.

- Don't worry about what order you fill the blanks in.

- Double check that once you've completed the question – your answers are grammatically and stylistically compatible.

Text Completion Examples

Directions: Choose one entry from the choices column for each blank. Fill in all blanks to finish the text best.

Text Completion Example 1

This question has three blanks:

It is refreshing to read a book about our planet by an author who does not allow facts to be

(i)_____ by politics: well aware of the political disputes about the effects of human activities on climate and biodiversity, this author does not permit them to (ii)_____ his comprehensive description of what we know about our biosphere. He emphasizes the enormous gaps in our knowledge, the sparseness of our observations, and the

(iii) _____, calling attention to the many aspects of planetary evolution that must be better understood before we can accurately diagnose the condition of our planet.

Blank (i)

Blank (ii)

Blank (iii)

    (A) overshadowed

    (B) invalidated

    (C) illuminated

    (D) enhance

    (E) obscure

    (F) underscore

    (G) plausibility of our hypotheses

    (H) certainty of our entitlement

    (I) superficiality of our theories

Explanation for Text Completion Example 1

The overall tone of the passage is clearly complimentary. To understand what the author of the book is being complimented on, it is useful to focus on the second blank. Here, we must determine what word would indicate something that the author is praised for not permitting. The only answer choice that fits the case is "obscure" (choice E), since enhancing and underscoring are generally good things to do, not things one should refrain from doing. Choosing "obscure" clarifies the choice for the first blank; the only choice that fits well with "obscure" is "overshadowed" (choice A). Notice that trying to fill blank

(i) without filling blank

(ii) first is very hard—each choice has at least some initial plausibility.

Since the third blank requires a phrase that matches "enormous gaps" and "sparseness of our observations," the best choice is "superficiality of our theories" (choice I). Thus the correct choices for the three blanks are overshadowed, obscure, and superficiality of our theories (choices A, E, and I). The correct completed text is:

It is refreshing to read a book about our planet by an author who does not allow facts to be overshadowed by politics: well aware of the political disputes about the effects of human activities on climate and biodiversity, this author does not permit them to obscure his comprehensive description of what we know about our biosphere. He emphasizes the enormous gaps in our knowledge, the sparseness of our observations, and the superficiality of our theories, calling attention to the many aspects of planetary evolution that must be better understood before we can accurately diagnose the condition of our planet.

Text Completion Example 2

This question has two blanks:

Vain and prone to violence, Caravaggio could not handle success: the more his _____ as an artist increased, the more _____ his life became.

Blank (i) Blank (ii)

    A. temperance D. tumultuous

    B. notoriety E. providential

    C. eminence F. dispassionate

Explanation for Text Completion Example 2

In this sentence, what follows the colon must explain or spell out what precedes it. So, roughly, what the second part must say is that as Caravaggio became more successful, his life got more out of control. When one looks for words to fill the blanks, it becomes clear that "tumultuous" (choice D) is the best fit for blank (ii), since neither of the other choices suggests being out of control. And for blank (i), the best choice is "eminence" (choice C), since to increase in eminence is a consequence of becoming more successful. It is true that Caravaggio might also increase in notoriety, but an increase in notoriety as an artist is not as clear a sign of success as an increase in eminence.

Thus the correct answer is eminence and tumultuous (choices C and D). The correct completed text is:

Vain and prone to violence, Caravaggio could not handle success: the more his eminence as an artist increased, the more tumultuous his life became.

Text Completion Example 3

This question has one blank:

In parts of the Arctic, the land grades into the land fast ice so _____ that you can walk off the coast and not know you are over the hidden sea.

    (A) permanently

    (B) imperceptibly

    (C) irregularly

    (D) precariously

    (E) relentlessly

Explanation for Text Completion Example 3

The word that fills the blank has to characterize how the land grades into the ice in a way that explains how you can walk off the coast and over the sea without knowing it. The word that does that is "imperceptibly" (choice B); if the land grades imperceptibly into the ice, you might well not know that you had left the land. Describing the shift from land to ice as permanent, irregular, precarious, or relentless would not help to explain how you would fail to know.

The correct completed text is:

In parts of the Arctic, the land grades into the land fast ice so imperceptibly that you can walk off the coast and not know you are over the hidden sea.

Sentence Equivalence Questions

Like Text Completion questions, Sentence Equivalence questions test the ability to reach a conclusion about how a passage should be completed on the basis of partial information, but to a greater extent, they focus on the meaning of the completed whole. Sentence Equivalence questions consist of a single sentence with just one blank, and they ask you to find two choices that both lead to a complete, coherent sentence and that produce sentences that mean the same thing.

Sentence Equivalence Question Structure

Each Sentence Equivalence question consists of:

- A single sentence

- One blank

- Six answer choices

Each question of this type requires you to select two of the answer choices; there is no credit for partially correct answers.

Answering Sentence Equivalence Questions Tips don't just search for two words saying the same thing in the responses. In two factors, that can be confusing. First, the answer choices can include pairs of terms that mean the same thing but do not match the sentence correctly, and thus do not constitute a correct answer. Third, the pair of terms that represent the right answer may not mean precisely the same thing, because the corresponding sentences say the same thing.

- Read the paragraph with an overarching meaning.

- Recognize terms or phrases that seem especially important, either because they reinforce the sentence structure (words like "except" or "over") or because they are central to communicating what the expression is about.

- Try to fill in the void for a word that you think suits to see if two related terms are given in the solution choices. When you see a term that's close to what you're thinking but can't locate a second one, don't correct that interpretation; then, see whether there are any vocabulary that can be found to fill the void reliably.

- When you have chosen your blank answer options, make sure that each sentence is objectively, grammatically and stylistically consistent, and that both sentences mean the same thing.

Directions: Choose the two solution options that, when used to complete the sentence, match the context of the sentence as a whole and yield equally valid completed sentences.

Sentence Equivalence Example 1

Although it does contain some pioneering ideas, one would hardly characterize the work as _____.

    (A) orthodox

    (B) eccentric

    (C) original

    (D) trifling

    (E) conventional

    (F) innovative

Explanation for Sentence Equivalence Example 1

The word "Although" is a crucial signpost here. The work contains some pioneering ideas, but apparently it is not overall a pioneering work. Thus the two words that could fill the blank appropriately are "original" (choice C) and "innovative" (choice F). Note that "orthodox" (choice A) and "conventional" (choice E) are two words that are very similar in meaning, but neither one completes the sentence sensibly.

Sentence Equivalence Example 2

It was her view that the country's problems had been _____ by foreign technocrats, so that to ask for such assistance again would be counterproductive.

    (A) ameliorated

    (B) ascertained

    (C) diagnosed

    (D) exacerbated

    (E) overlooked

    (F) worsened

Explanation for Sentence Equivalence Example 2

The sentence relates a piece of reasoning, as indicated by the presence of "so that": asking for the assistance of foreign technocrats would be counterproductive because of the effects such technocrats have had already. This means that the technocrats must have had bad effects; that is, they must have "exacerbated" (choice D) or "worsened" (choice F) the country's problems.

GRE Quantitative Reasoning

The sort of math on the GRE is like the math that you studied in your sophomore year or junior high school. You may have forgotten a lot – if not all – of these things like: standard form, geometric properties (circles, quadrilaterals, etc.), integer properties, and exponents, word problems (including concentrations and probability).

That which makes the GRE so difficult is the difficulty and impenetrability of certain problems.

The best part about it is that you don't need to show your working out, like you did at school, you need to simply pick the right answer.

The GRE geometry checks your ability to calculate basic mathematical problems and your geometrical understanding. Yet it also checks how you handle problem solving. The GRE math section checks the ability to think with numbers. Sometimes, the trick to answering a query is to objectively unwrap the dilemma, not just crunch a lot of numbers. It requires you to pull the information you need, out of a question.

The GRE Quantitative section is broken up into Problem Solving questions and Quantitative Comparison (QC) questions. The math section will always begin with either seven or eight QC questions. For each QC question you must compare two columns, A and B, to determine which one is bigger.

The Problem Solving section consists of up to five-answer multiple-choice questions, multiple-answer questions, and Numeric Entry questions. Numeric Entry questions have no answer choices. You must type your answer into a box.

Quantitative Comparison, Problem Solving, and Numeric Entry can all test you on various math concepts (Geometry, Probability, etc.). See the chart below for more info on the subjects the GRE tests.

The questions are designed to annoy you. The incorrect responses are not arbitrarily selected either; Exam designers know just how students get confused by questions — and they may have the "correct" responses ready to catch you, unless you're cautious. Sometimes the question seems so easy, so you fly through it without realising you've fallen for a trick. Watch out if a question seems straightforward and you're less likely to get caught. That's, you'll learn to find traps by spending a bit more time. This skill is a "trick.

Other "tricks" include estimation, which can help you hone in on the correct answer, without having to resort to the calculator. The calculator can be helpful but it can also slow you down and allow you to make mistakes in typing. For example, if you have to convert the fraction 181/502 into a percentage, note how 18/50 is a very close approximation. 18/50 is the same as 36/100, which is 36%. Questions of this nature often ask for an approximation. Additionally, the answer choices are spaced far apart, meaning you won't have (A) 36% (B) 39%. So feel free to shave a little off fractions, just like I did.

Most people assume that by getting a maths book and doing more calculations and covering more concepts they will improve their mathematics. Real practice, initial learning formulas and lots of mathematic background would naturally make a big difference. But you need to be careful for mistakes. For one, you could slip into an ETS loop. For example, in Quantitative Analysis, its pretty easy to get the wrong answer if you just checked a few figures. So learning to be prepared and alert could make much more of a difference than reading three hours on math basics.

Most of the GRE Quantitative section battle is studying tactics and adapting them to more challenging problems. In other words, when you start working north of the 150 range, tactics and definitions don't change — the challenges just get harder.

You have to do more complicated problems to train yourself properly. Education is intellectual. Students who think math isn't nice may conclude that every problem they answer is a confirmation of this reality. The more likely explanation is whether their talents are outdated or those abilities were never properly nurtured first. If you fall into this category, you will need to do lots and lots of mathematics practice in order to prepare. Get your skills up to date and fresh.

After this you need two crucial things: endurance and determination.

GRE Mathematical Mastery won't come overnight, much like when you were at school; you'll progress a little at a time. Training plateaus will feel so lengthy you'll think you've reached the proverbial brick wall. That's when patience becomes a virtue... And be on guard against that voice in the back of your head who wants to keep saying, "I'm not a math person." So may say this then end up scoring better in math than the Verbal.

I now have a load of examples of the type of questions you will face.

GRE Quantitative Reasoning Examples

Quantitative Reasoning

Because GRE math checks your ability to solve problems; you do need a wealth of math formulas at your fingertips. While it might seem really overwhelming, in a few pages, the amount of formulas you need to learn will really help you in the exam. This doesn't mean the abundance of calculations that you used to have for when you were at school, however.

Formula Sheet

While the GRE isn't really a test of wrote knowledge, more an ability to think on the day. You will need to show up on test day with just some important facts memorized. Unlike some other standardized tests, there is no "cheat sheet" of mathematical formulas included. This means you need to commit around a dozen to memory; some you'll certainly recall from high school geometry, and others that may be unfamiliar.

Let's start with the easy stuff:

Geometry Formulas

Circles (Let r = radius and d = diameter)

Area: $A = \pi r2$

Circumference: $C = \pi (2r)$ or Pd

Squares (Let s = side length)

Area: s2

Perimeter: 4s

Rectangles (Let L = length and W = width)

Area: L x W

Perimeter: 2L + 2W

Triangles (Let b = base and h = height)

Area: 1/2bh

Trapezoids (a = top parallel side, b = bottom parallel side, h = height)

Area :(a+b)/2 x h

Slope

y=mx + b

The steepness of a line on the coordinate plane can be calculated using the slope formula. The b is where the line crosses the y-axis, and is called the "y-intercept." The x and y can be any point along the line; you'll always have these three numbers. Simply solve for y to get your m.

Distance, rate, time

d = rt

The GRE loves distance = rate x time problems and you'll definitely see them on the test. As long as you have two of the variables—and you always will—you can derive the third. Test gives you time and distance and asks you for rate? Divide both sides by t so that your equation is now r = d/t.

Interest rate

Simple interest is the type of interest where the rate of growth is always applied to the original principal. Let p = principal, r = rate, and t = time

$V = P [1+(r/100n)]$

Compound interest is when the rate of growth is applied to the current principal. Let n = number of times compounded annually.

$V = P [1+(r/100n)]^{nt}$

No matter what your GRE study strategy looks like, be sure to have these formulas committed to memory before test day.

To combat the no-formula terror, write down a few formulas at the beginning of the section — especially those that you find hard to think up on the spot. Yes, it can cost you 30 seconds, but frantically attempting to retrieve the formula for the volume of a sphere can cause you to forget the problem – and lose your flow.

GRE Quantitative Reasoning Examples

Practice for GRE Quantitative Comparison Questions

Quantitative comparison questions ask you to compare Quantity 1 to Quantity 2. You need to compare the two and decide which of the following describes the relationship:

Quantity 1 is greater.

Quantity 2 is greater.

The two quantities are equal.

The relationship cannot be determined from the information given.

1. The average (arithmetic mean) high temperature for x days is 60 degrees. The addition of one day with a high temperature of 65 degrees increases the average to 61 degrees.

Quantity A	Quantity B
x	5

(A) Quantity A is greater.

(B) Quantity B is greater.

(C) The two quantities are equal.

(D) The relationship cannot be determined from the information given.

Answer: (B) Quantity B is greater.

If the average high temperature for x days is 60 degrees, then the sum of those x high temperatures is 60x. The sum of the high temperatures, including the additional day that has a temperature of 65 degrees is, therefore, 60x + 65. Next, use the average formula to find the value of x:

In this formula, 61 is the average, 60x + 65 is the total, and there are x + 1 days. Substituting this information into the formula gives:

To solve, cross-multiply to get 61x + 61 = 60x + 65. Next, simplify to find that x = 4. Therefore, Quantity B is greater. The correct answer is (B).

2. c and d are integers.

$c^2 = d^3$

Quantity A	Quantity B
c	d

(A) Quantity A is greater.

(B) Quantity B is greater.

(C) The two quantities are equal.

(D) The relationship cannot be determined from the information given.

Answer: (D) The relationship cannot be determined from the information given.

Try different integers for c and d that satisfy the equation $c^2 = d^3$ such as c = 8 and d = 3. These numbers satisfy the equation as $8^2 = 4^3 = 64$. In this case, Quantity A is greater. Because Quantity B is not always greater nor are the two quantities always equal, choices (B) and (C) can be eliminated. Next, try some different numbers. When choosing a second set of numbers, try something less common such as making c = d = 1. Again, these numbers satisfy the equation provided in the problem. In this case, however, the quantities are equal. Because Quantity A is not always greater, choice (A) can now be eliminated. The correct answer is (D).

For question 3, select one answer from the list of five answer choices.

3. A certain Shoe store sells only brown shoes and black shoes. In March, the store sold twice as many brown shoes as black shoes. In April, the store sold twice the number of brown shoes that it sold in March, and three times the number of black shoes that it sold in March. If the total number of Shoes the store sold in March and April combined was 500, how many brown shoes did the store sell in March?

(A) 80

(B) 100

(C) 120

(D) 160

(E) 180

Answer: (B) 100

Plug in the Answers, starting with the middle choice. If 120 brown shoes were sold in March, then 60 black shoes were sold that month. In April, 240 brown shoes were sold, along with 180 black shoes. The total number of brown shoes and black shoes sold during those two months is 600, which is too large, so eliminate (C), (D), and (E). Try (B). If there were 100 brown shoes sold in March, then 50 black shoes were sold; in April, 200 brown shoes were sold along with 150 black shoes. The correct answer is (B) because 100 + 50 + 200 + 150 = 500.

4. Triangle ABC has an area of 108 cm 2. If both x and y are integers, which of the following could be the value of x?

Indicate all such values.

    (A) 4

    (B) 5

    (C) 6

    (D) 8

    (E) 9

Answer: (A), (C), (D) and (E)

Plug the information given into the formula for the area of a triangle to learn more about the relationship between x and y: The product of x and y is 216, so x needs to be a factor of 216. The only number in the answer choices that is not a factor of 216 is 5. The remaining choices are possible values of x.

Exercise set 1.

1. What is the area of the Triangle ACL Below?

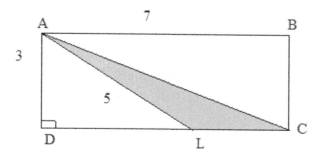

(A) 2.5

(B) 3

(C) 3.5

(D) 4

(E) 4.5

2. Paul has two more than twice as many chocolates as does Amy, and half as many chocolates as does Nigel. If Amy has 'a' number of chocolates, then in terms of 'a', how many chocolates do Paul, Amy and Nigel have?

(A) 2a+ 4

(B) 5a+5

(C) 6a+7

(D) 7a+6

(E) 9a+4

3. Oil needs to be thinned to a ratio of 3 parts oil to 2 parts water. The oil owner has by mistake added water so that he has 8 litres of oil which is half water and half oil. What must he add to make the proportions of the mixture correct?

4. The width of a rectangle is 2/3 times its length. If the length is calculated to be 9, what is the value of perimeter for this rectangle?

5. A line l is parallel to the y-axis and passes through the point (2, 3). What is its gradient (m) and x-intercept?

(A) m= 0, x= (3, 0)

(B) m= ∞, x= (2, 0)

(C) m= 0, x= (2, 0)

(D) m= ∞, x= (3, 0)

(E) m= 2, x= (0, 0)

6. What is the equation of the new parabola created by shifting $y = x^2$, three units in the positive y-axis direction?

(A) $y = (x+3)^2$

(B) $y = x^2$

(C) $y = x^2 + 3$

(D) $3y = x^2$

(E) $y = x^3$

7. A sphere with diameter 1 unit is enclosed in a cube of side 1 unit each. Find the unoccupied volume remaining inside the cube.

(A) ¼

(B) 2π

(C) $\pi/6-1$

(D) $1-\pi/4$

(E) $1-\pi/6$

8. The function $y=4x^2$ is moved 2 units upwards on the positive x-axis (right) and 3 units towards the positive y-axis (up). Find the resulting function.

(A) $y=4x^2+5$

(B) $y=4x^2$

(C) $y=4(x+2)2+3$

(D) $y=4(x-2)2-3$

(E) y=4(x-2)2+3

9. Find the shaded area when two squares with side 'a' intersect as shown in the figure below.

(A) 1/8 a^2

(B) 1/4 a^2

(C) a^2

(D) 1/3 a^2

(E) 2/5 a^2

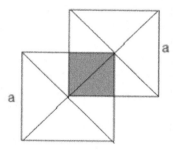

10. If the largest side of a triangle is A and the other two sides are B and C. What relation exists between them?

(A) A=B+C

(B) A+C

(C) A>|B-C|

(D) |B-C|

(E) A=π(B-C)

Exercise set 2

1. A mixed team of four young researchers is to be chosen from a group of 7 male and 5 female students.

Quantity A	Quantity B
The number of different research teams with 3 female students and 1 male student	66

Quantity A is greater

Quantity B is greater

Both Quantities are equal

The relationship cannot be determined

2. Line segment AB and Line segment CD are parallel to each other, such that the lines which are intersecting these two line segments are also parallel to each other.

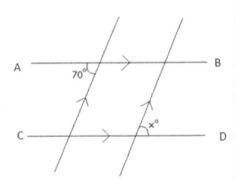

Quantity A	Quantity B
70 Degrees	X

(A) Quantity A is greater

(B) Quantity B is greater

(C) Both Quantities are equal

(D) The relationship cannot be determined

3. In a particular Zoo, there are 30 animals, such that 14 of these animals like to eat white meat, whereas 13 animals like to eat grains. 9 animals are neither fond of white meat nor grains.

Quantity A	Quantity B
The number of animals which eat both white meat and grains.	

(A) Quantity A is greater

(B) Quantity B is greater

(C) Both Quantities are equal

(D) The relationship cannot be determined

4. Chose the correct answer from the given quantities.

Quantity A	Quantity B
124 + 376 + 539	129 + 397 + 543

(A) Quantity A is greater

(B) Quantity B is greater

(C) Both Quantities are equal

(D) The relationship cannot be determined

5. The average arithmetic mean of 5 numbers is 100. From this given information, chose the correct option.

Quantity A	Quantity B
Sum of these numbers	133

(A) Quantity A is greater

(B) Quantity B is greater

(C) Both Quantities are equal

(D) The relationship cannot be determined

6. A + B = 3 and A − B = 4. From the given information, chose the correct option.

Quantity A	Quantity B

A   B

(A) Quantity A is greater

(B) Quantity B is greater

(C) Both Quantities are equal

(D) The relationship cannot be determined

7. At a firework company, the ratio of male employees to female employees was 8 to 9. After some time, 10 more employees were hired such that 6 were male and 4 were female.

Quantity A   Quantity B

The number of male employees   The number of female
after recruitment   employees after recruitment

(A) Quantity A is greater

(B) Quantity B is greater

(C) Both Quantities are equal

(D) The relationship cannot be determined

8. Select the correct option.

Quantity A   Quantity B

164   123

(A) Quantity A is greater

(B) Quantity B is greater

(C) Both Quantities are equal

(D) The relationship cannot be determined

9. If x+2y= 4 and x+3y= 9. Find the correct option.

Quantity A	Quantity B
X	y

(A) Quantity A is greater

(B) Quantity B is greater

(C) Both Quantities are equal

(D) The relationship cannot be determined

10. If $x^2+ 2x-5=10$, select the correct option.

Quantity A	Quantity B
3	x

(A) Quantity A is greater

(B) Quantity B is greater

(C) Both Quantities are equal

(D) The relationship cannot be determined

Exercise set 3.

Directions: Write your answer into the box provided. Do not use units or special characters (e.g., $, feet, etc.). If answer is a fraction, enter in simplest form (i.e., 3/4 vs. 6/8) - please note that on the computer exam this will be "please write"

1. During a college fundraiser, the entrance fee for students was $12 and for teachers (and their family members) it was $30. 75 people came to attend that event and a total of $1800 was gathered. How many students came to this fundraiser?

2. In a certain society, the ratio of unemployed people to employed people is 2:5 respectively. If there are 700 employed people in that society, how many are unemployed?

3. The date of birth of Randy is November 3rd, 1920. After living a successful life as a politician, she died on April 24th, 1983. What was her age in years when she died?

4. Nigel and Isa started a new company and decided that the net profit will be divided in a 6:7 ratio respectively. At the end of first month, they got a profit of $390. What is the amount that Nigel got after the first month?

5. Consider the following two equations and find the value of $x - 3y$.

$2x-4y= 4$

$x - y = 3$

6. What is the probability that two of your friends were born on the same day of the week?

Answer as a fraction (e.g., 3/5 or 4/6)

7. There are 'x' balls in blue bag and the number of balls in green bag are '2x'. The average price of balls in blue bag is $20 and the average price of balls of green bag is $30. If all the balls of these two bags are put in a yellow bag, what would be the average price of balls of yellow bag?

Round to the nearest tenth (e.g., 23.7 or 18.6)

8. In a 3.5 hours long board game session, Amy scored 525 points. How many points did she score per minute?

10. In a Mathematics test, out of total 25 questions, Nigel left questions 5 to 13 blank. How many questions did he attempt?

Exercise set 4

1. Given that a/b = 1/6 and 9a-b = 12, which of the following is greater than 'b'. Indicate all the possible answers.

    (A) 25

    (B) 28

    (C) 20

    (D) 19

    (E) 1

2. Which of the following represent the sum of two integers such that the product of these two integers is 12? Indicate all the possible answers.

    (A) -8

    (B) 7

    (C) 13

    (D) 1

3. Answer the question below:

    (A) 15

    (B) 13

    (C) 12

    (D) 19

4. Paul went out to a supermarket to buy some house hold items. He bought a total of 4 items. The average price of first three items is $100. What was the price of 4th item if the overall average of these four items is less than $105 and greater than $95?

    (A) 77

    (B) 2

    (C) 84

    (D) 88

    (E) 115

(F) 198

5. Which of the following options are smaller than the arithmetic mean of prime factors of 22? Indicate all possible options.

(A) 3

(B) 5

(C) 9

(D) 11

(E) 13

6. Let 'x' and 'y' be two integers such that $x < 0$ and $y < 0$. Which of the following options could values of $xy/(x+y)$. Indicate all possible options.

(A) 1

(B) -27

(C) -7

(D) 4

(E) 6

Exercise set 1. Answers

1. What is the area of triangle ALC in the figure given below?

Correct answer is: 4.5

Explanation: First of all, we need to find LC, but for that, we need to find DL. We know that AB= DC = 7.

So, LC = DC- DL

Now, DL = √ (5^2- 3^2) = 4 (using Pythagoras Theorem)

So, LC = 7-4 = 3

Therefore, Area = (1/2) (Base) (Height) = (0.5) (3) (3) = 4.5

Explanation: First of all, we need to find LC, but for that, we need to find DL. We know that AB= DC = 7.

So, LC = DC- DL

Now, DL = 4 (using Pythagoras Theorem)

So, LC = 7-4 = 3

Therefore, Area = (1/2) (Base) (Altitude) = (0.5) (3) (3) = 4.5

2. Paul has two more than twice as many chocolates as does Amy, and half as many chocolates as does Nigel. If Amy has 'a' number of chocolates, then in terms of 'a', how many chocolates do Alan, Amy and Nigel have?

Correct answer is: 7a+6

Explanation: We know that Amy has 'a' chocolates. Paul has 2a+2 chocolates from the given statement in the question. Nigel has double the chocolates as Paul has, so she has 4a+4 chocolates.

Adding these, we get 4a+4+2a+2+a = 7a +6. So, Option (d) is correct.

3. Oil needs to be thinned to a ratio of 3 parts oil to 2 parts water. The oil owner has by mistake added water so that he has 8 liters of oil which is half water and half oil. What must he add to make the proportions of the mixture correct?

Correct answer is: 2 liters oil

Explanation: We note that the final ratio must be 3:2 for oil and water respectively. Now, according to given scenario in the question, we have eight liters of solution with 4 liters oil and 4 liters water, which makes it 2:2. In order to make it 3:2, we add 2 liters oil. This would make a total of 6 liters oil and 4 liters water i.e. 6:4 which can be simplified to 3:2.

4. The width of a rectangle is 2/3 times its length. If the length is calculated to be 9, what is the value of perimeter for this rectangle?

Correct answer is: 30

Explanation: As the width of the rectangle is 2/3 times its length which is 9, the width comes out to be 6. Therefore, the perimeter becomes, 6+6+9+9 = 30. (Perimeter of a rectangle is calculated by adding the lengths of each side of that rectangle)

5. A line l is parallel to the y-axis and passes through the point (2, 3). What is its gradient (m) and x-intercept?

Correct answer is: m= ∞, x= (2, 0)

Explanation: As the given line is parallel to the y-axis, and the slope of y-axis is infinite, therefore its slope is also infinite. As the line is defined by x=2, hence its x intercept will also be 2 because all of its points will be of the form (2, y).

6. C was correct.

Explanation: As the parabola is shifted above, the change would come in the value of y, so we increase y i.e. the whole function by 3 units. Therefore, y=x2+3

7. A sphere with diameter 1 unit is enclosed in a cube of side 1 unit each. Find the unoccupied volume remaining inside the cube.

Correct answer is: 1-π/6

Explanation: We find the volume of the cube by the formula $length^3$. We then subtract from it the volume of the sphere to find the empty volume. The volume of cube amounts to 1x1x1=1. The volume of the sphere is (4/3) x π x $(radius)^3$. Putting in the values we get (4/3) x π x $(0.5)^3$. This is equal to π/6. Subtracting the two gives 1- π/6.

8. Explanation: The upward shift is simply addressed by adding three in the given function, and the horizontal shift is addressed by changing the value of x in the given function. If the shift is a units towards right, then we replace x with x-a. If the shift is towards left then we replace x with x+a.

9. Explanation: We realize that the shaded figure is actually a square of side 0.5a. The answer follows, area=0.5a x 0.5a=0.25a². (Area of a square of side a is a²)

10. If the largest side of a triangle is A and the other two sides are B and C. What relation exists between them?

The answer of |B-C| was correct.

Explanation: The largest side is greater than the difference of the smaller sides and less than the sum of the two smaller sides

Exercise set 2 Answers

1. A mixed team of four young researchers is to be chosen from a group of 7 male and 5 female students.

Your answer of was incorrect.

Correct answer is: Quantity A is greater

Explanation: Start off by finding the number of groups which can be formed having 3 females out of 5. i.e. $(5x4x3)/(3x2x1) = 10$. Now, we multiply it by the total number of male students who can be coupled in to form a group of total four members. Therefore, $10x7 = 70$.

As $70 > 66$, The correct answer is therefore A.

2. Line segment AB and Line segment CD are parallel to each other, such that the lines which are intersecting these two line segments are also parallel to each other.

Correct answer is: Both Quantities are equal

Explanation: When parallel lines are intersected by parallel lines, the opposite angles are always equal. If we look closely, we see that the given angle 70 degrees becomes opposite angle to unknown angle 'x', and therefore, these two are equal.

3. In a particular Zoo, there are 30 animals, such that 14 of these animals like to eat white meat, whereas 13 animals like to eat grains. 9 animals are neither fond of white meat nor grains.

Correct answer is: Quantity B is greater

Explanation: The easiest and the most time efficient way to solve these group questions is to simply substitute the value in the formula i.e.

Total = Group 1 + Group 2 – Both + Neither

30 = 14 + 13 – Both + 9

Both = 6

So, the animals which eat both kinds of food are 6.

We chose option B as our correct answer.

4. Chose the correct answer from the given quantities.

Correct answer is: Quantity B is greater

Explanation: This is a simple question but most of the candidates will waste their time on this type of question by adding all numbers and then comparing. However, you need to save your time in these types of questions. You note that all the numbers in quantity B are greater than respective numbers in quantity A so you don't need to add the numbers. Therefore, option (B) is correct.

5. The average arithmetic mean of 5 numbers is 100. From this given information, chose the correct option.

Your answer of was incorrect.

Correct answer is: Quantity A is greater

Explanation: Now let's read the given information once again carefully. We know that arithmetic mean of 5 numbers equals the sum of those 5 numbers divided by 5. Now, we have the arithmetic mean equal to 100 as given. This means that, sum of these numbers is $100*5 = 500$.

Now we know that $500 > 133$, so we chose option (a).

6. $A + B = 3$ and $A - B = 4$. From the given information, chose the correct option.

Your answer of was incorrect.

Correct answer is: Quantity A is greater

Explanation: In order to solve this question, you have to find the values of A and B. From first equation, we get to know that $A = 3 - B$. So we put this value of A in second equation, which becomes, $3- B - B = 4$, solving this equation, we get $-2B = 1$ i.e. $B= -1/2$. And $A = 7/2$. So option (a) is correct.

7. At a firework company, the ratio of male employees to female employees was 8 to 9. After some time, 10 more employees were hired such that 6 were male and 4 were female.

Correct answer is: The relationship cannot be determined

Explanation: As given in the statement of the question, the ratio of male to female employees was 8 to 9 which means that if there were 8 male, there were 9 female. Similarly, for 16 male, there would be18 female or we can say that for 24 male, there would be 27 female. Now after the hiring process was complete, 6 male and 4 female were hired, which could make the total 14 male and 13 female, or maybe 22 male and 22 female, or maybe 30 male and 31 female. As the total number of employees is not given, we can't be sure which of these is correct. Therefore, we select option D.

9. If x+2y= 4 and x+3y= 9. Find the correct option.

Correct answer is: Quantity B is greater

Explanation: In order to find the correct option, we need to find the values of x and y. We know from first equation that x= 4- 2y. Putting this value of x in second equation, we get, 4-2y+3y = 9 i.e. y = 5. And x= 4 – 2(5) = -6.

So, y>x. Therefore, Quantity B > Quantity A.

10. If $x^2 + 2x-5=10$, select the correct option.

Quantity A	Quantity B
3	x

Quantity A is greater

Quantity B is greater

Both Quantities are equal

The relationship cannot be determined

You need to solve the equation for x, in this case using the formula $x = \frac{-b \pm \sqrt{(b^2-4ac)}}{2a}$ in order to find that x could be -5 or x could be 3. As we don't know which of the 2 possible values it is going to be, the relationship cannot be determined.

Exercise set 3 Answers

1. Answer the question below:

During a college fundraiser, the entrance fee for students was $12 and for teachers (and their family members) it was $30. 75 people came to attend that event and a total of $1800 was gathered. How many students came to this fundraiser?

Correct answer is: 25

Explanation:

Let x be the number of students

Number of teachers = 75 − x

$12 \times x + 30 \times (75 - x) = 1800$

$12x + 2250 - 30x = 1800$

$18x = 450$

$x = 25$

Therefore, the number of students who attended this event = 25

2. In a certain society, the ratio of unemployed people to employed people is 2:5 respectively. If there are 700 employed people in that society, how many are unemployed?

Correct answer is: 280

Explanation: In order to find the solution to this question, we write the given data in form of a mathematical equation i.e. $2/5 = x/700$

Where 'x' is the number of unemployed people. Solving this equation, we get to know that x= (2x700)/5 = 1400/5= 280

3. The date of birth of Randy is November 3rd, 1920. After living a successful life as a politician, she died on April 24th, 1983. What was her age in years when she died?

Correct answer is: 62

Explanation: The last birthday of Randy was in the year 1982. So, her age at the time of her death was 1982-1920 = 62 years

4. Nigel and Isa started a new company and decided that the net profit will be divided in a 6:7 ratio respectively. At the end of first month, they got a profit of $390. What is the amount that Nigel got after the first month?

Correct answer is: 180

Explanation: In order to solve this question, you simply need to know the value of each single part i.e. 390/13 = $30 Therefore, total profit for Nigel is 6 x 30 = $180.

5. Consider the following two equations and find the value of x – 3y.

Correct answer is: 1

Explanation: In order to find the correct answer, we need to find the values of x and y. Simplifying first equation, it becomes, x-2y= 2. From second equation, we note that x= 3+y. Putting this value in simplified version of first equation, we get, 3+y-2y=2 -> -y=-1 -> y=1.

And, x= 3+y = 4.

So, x - 3y = 4 - 3= 1

6. What is the probability that two of your friends were born on the same day of the week?

Correct answer is: 1/7

Explanation: This looks like a relatively easy question but many students get confused in answering these types of questions. You must not be confused with 'two friends'. The probability is simple as 1/7 i.e. 7 days of week.

7. Correct answer is: 26.7

Explanation: In order to find the average price, we multiply the average of each group by its size and add the results. i.e. (20x1) + (30x2)= 20+60 = 80. Now we have the total number of balls. If we divide it by total size (i.e. x+2x= 3x), we will get the overall average.

Therefore, 80/3 = 26.66 = 26.7 approx.

8. In a 3.5 hours long board game session, Amy scored 525 points. How many points did she score per minute?

Correct answer is: 2.5

Explanation: First we convert 3.5 hours to minutes, i.e., we have 3.5x60= 210 minutes. So, 525/210 equals 2.5 points per minute.

9. In a Mathematics test, out of total 25 questions, Nigel left questions 5 to 13 blank. How many questions did he attempt?

Correct answer is: 16

Explanation: You simply need to count the number of questions that he left and then subtract that from the total number of questions. I.e. 25-9 = 16

5 to 13 means that he left question number 5,6,7,8,9,10,11,12,13 i.e. total 9 questions left.

10.0Answer the following question:

Given that a/b = 1/6 and 9a-b = 12, which of the following is greater than 'b'. Indicate all the possible answers.

Correct answer is: 25 28

Explanation: a/b = 1/6 means b= 6a. Putting this in the other equation, we get 9a-6a = 12

-> 3a =12 -> a=4

9(4) – b = 12 -> 36-12 = b -> b= 24

Only options (e,f) are greater than 24.

Exercise set 4 Answers

1. Given that a/b = 1/6 and 9a-b = 12, which of the following is greater than 'b'. Indicate all the possible answers.

25

28

20

19

1

Explanation: a/b = 1/6 means b= 6a. Putting this in the other equation, we get 9a-6a = 12

Therefore 3a =12

Hence a=4

Subbing into other equation gives

9(4) – b = 12 -> 36-12 = b -> b= 24

Only options 25 and 28 are greater than 24

2. Which of the following represent the sum of two integers such that the product of these two integers is 12? Indicate all the possible answers.

-8

7

13

1

Correct answer is: -8 7 13

Explanation: First of all, we note that we can get 12 by multiplying 1 with 12, 2 with 6, and 3 with 4. Similarly, multiplying the negative of these numbers also yields the same results. Therefore, the sums of these numbers could be 13, 8, 7, -13, -8, and -7.

3. Answer the question below:

15

13

12

19

Explanation: The least number of biscuit brands are 15. Also, the ratio of chocolate brands to biscuit brands is 3: 5. Therefore, 3/5= x/15 x=9 where 'x' is the minimum number of chocolate brands. It is possible that there are more than 15 brands of biscuits and thus, the possibility of more than 9 chocolate brands.

Correct answer is: 12 15 19

4. Paul went out to a supermarket to buy some house hold items. He bought a total of 4 items. The average price of first three items is $100. What was the price of 4th item if the overall average of these four items is less than $105 and greater than $95?

77

2

84

88

115

198

Your answer of was incorrect.

Correct answer is: 84 88 115

Explanation: Lets these four items be W, X, Y, Z. Now, (w+x+y)/3=100 -> w+x+y = 300

Now, 95<(w+x+y+z)/4<105 -> 380< w+x+y+z <420

And w+x+y is 300 (calculated in the first step). So, the equation becomes, $80 < z < $120.

5. Which of the following options are smaller than the arithmetic mean of prime factors of 22? Indicate all possible options.

3

5

9

11

13

Explanation: The prime factors of 22 are 2 and 11. Their average becomes (2+11)/2 = 6.5

Only options A and B are smaller than 6.5.

6. Let 'x' and 'y' be two integers such that x < 0 and y < 0. Which of the following options could values of xy/(x+y). Indicate all possible options.

1

-27

-7

4

6

Explanation: Some of the students might get confused while answering this question. However, the basic concept is very simple. As mentioned in the question, both x and y are negative integers (x < 0, y < 0) as we know that the product of two negative integers is positive, so the numerator becomes positive. The sum of two negative integers is always negative, so the denominator becomes negative. Hence, the overall fraction becomes negative.

Correct answer is: -21 -7

Analytical Writing

Introduction to GRE Analytical Writing

"Having to learn more about the GRE segment of writing cannot just bring you a perfect score, but also help you become a stronger researcher" ... Achieving a 99 percentile score on any of the GRE parts takes several weeks, if not months, of persistence, dedication, practice, and smart planning. Yet you can comfortably get a 99 percentile score on the AWA segment with just a small percentage of the hard work you put in for Math and Verbal, and a few days of practice. If you manage this, your score WILL stand out.

Analytical writing is GRE's most overlooked area. Worldwide, test takers say they can quickly learn AWA in a day or two yet the AWA average score worldwide is just 4.0. The thing is that getting much higher, getting a 6.0 even, is very achievable!

When you're trying to score a perfect 6.0 on the AWA test, you'll have to be even more prepared than other students. Just as in the other two sections, mastering the GRE essay section takes the same amount of confidence, patience, and practice and hard work.

The GRE section of Analytical writing has two essays; each of these will be sat in 30 minutes or less. The two papers you'll see on GRE are, Issue and argument Analysis those two essays will always be important, no matter what. You can't just Miss AWA, go to other pages, and come back later. AWA itself is a different segment, so you can move forward only after completing the two essays.

I think that it's important to note that the AWA only tests how good you can write an article, therefore just testing your writing skills. Like common sense, the AWA doesn't examine the reasoning process. So long as the article sounds rational, then your ability to write is what it is testing.

It's a well-known reality that your AWA essay performance isn't as important as your GRE combined math and verbal performance, so having a 5.0 or 6.0 won't make or break the odds of being accepted to your preference university. Graduate school admissions officers just care with the AWA ranking if it's too low or lower than their normal class level. Sure, a bad AWA score will probably raise a red flag, and the admission committee would undoubtedly think twice before letting you in. They might also go back into your application documents to check that you really wrote them.

AWA ranking varies from 0 to 6.0, with 0.5 point increments. The system is set up to rate the answers to each of these essay questions on a 6-point scale, with 6 being the highest and 1, the lowest. The criteria that ETS looks for when assessing the AWA essays that score a 6.0 are:

Outstanding: a well-articulated attempt of successful writing and the ability to specifically define and examine the main features of the argument with profound insight. Develops cogent concepts, systematically organizes them, and integrates them without abrupt transformations. Strongly respects arguments key points. Demonstrates superior English language knowledge, including pronunciation, sentence formation, spelling, grammar and variation used in standard written English. No defects in the article.

Each of your AWA essays is ranked 0 to 6. Two readers will read your essay and give it a respectable grade, and two separate readers will read your essay and award it a grade. -- grader will give a 6.0 to top essays and 0 scores are reserved for essays written on subjects other than those given or written in a foreign language. The graders spend about 30 seconds to 2 minutes on each essay and assign it a score based on pre-defined assessment criteria like the overall quality of your critical thinking and writing, as previously mentioned. The graders assessing the answers are faculty members from different subject fields, including higher education.

After the essay is done, the two scores will be combined to achieve a final AWA ranking. Whether the scores provided by the two reviewers are more than one point apart, a third highly qualified grader is called in to overcome the difference (i.e. assess the final score for that essay).

For each essay, the final score is the average score given by the two readers or the third reader's adjusted ranking.

It should be remembered that while the AWA scores vary from 0-6, approximately 90 percent of all scores are between from 2 to 5. The overall AWA ranking for all test takers so far is around 4.2.

Your Writing Evaluation scores are measured and published separately from multiple-choice.

Some students believe that the most relevant element in AWA scores is how long it is.

The grade will look for several key areas:

1. Clarity this is the most critical and basic of all aspects on which the graders judge the essays. The grader will understand what you're trying to mean, read once. It makes their job harder, and they will realize that if it can be understood with just one reading, the article is straightforward.

As I said earlier they grader does not spend long on the paper, so they really don't want to read it twice, as such, make sure that it is clear what the topic is!

Content matters more than everything else that is in your essays. Therefore, make sure you have solid points and straightforward, easily understandable logical reasoning.

2. Structure:

Structure is the second most critical element in your essays. The formatting of a document influences its readability significantly. Your essays can read like a story; something that can be easily understood, and something that has a clear arrangement and structure. Therefore, it's important to divide your essay into separate paragraphs, each with its own meaning and context, while retaining a smooth transition from one paragraph to the next.

Every paragraph needs to read like a separate story, and the essay graders will quickly search through your whole document. Plus, as the transitions are seamless and there are no abrupt twists in your answers, it will make the grader's job much easier.

3. Sentence mixing

While writing multiple paragraphs on the same subject, you should preferably avoid writing similar the same sentences. If you're an ardent news reader, you will get the point. No good writer writes two precisely the same sentences in one essay or paragraph. Consecutive sentences of the same structure and duration can sound monotonous and bland, and most importantly they are clearly boring for the reader.

Instead of repetitive and dull sentences, use sentence structure skilfully. You don't have to rearrange the words, or chance the voice from passive to active, or vice-versa. It simply means you should use different words to mean the same thing.

For example if you've already written the term 'A leader's most valuable value is a good sense of ethics,' then if you want to say something similar later, you can attempt to rephrase the same word then write something like this: 'A clear moral foundation is crucial for any chief.'

By flipping between short and long sentences, you should keep changing sentence structures, flow and rhythm. You should also use intermediate and signal words to differentiate openings and ends.

4. Vocabulary

Among test takers, there's been a longstanding theory that the GRE really loves strong vocabulary, so using it on your essays can improve your performance.

Like I said earlier, AWA doesn't check how much vocabulary you have used. This is tested earlier in the exam; instead, AWA just checks how well you can get the information out of a text and write a fair critique of someone else's problem or argument. If you can use logic, correct syntax and intelligently justify your argument alongside using specific words to clearly express meaning, everything will be ok.

5. Language and Grammar

While officially ETS says you may have small errors in the essay file; it doesn't mean you should overlook mistakes. While mistakes or defects do not interfere with general sense and accuracy, you will realize that when you make the first mistake on the document, the grader will note it and be more aware when reading the remainder of the text. Then any more mistakes you make are even more apparent. Take enough time to make sure you are precise.

6. Logic

Logic is crucial in assessing the essay's overall content Find as much evidence as you can to back up what you say in your essay. One of the key characteristics of a convincing article is the potential to persuade the listener by strong logical thinking. Anyone who reads your answers should be completely persuaded of your point of view. With enough practice, you will be able to do this.

Nearly half of GRE test takers are English-speakers. Often they believe it's not worth wasting time in something they're really good at by birth right. However there are some flaw sin that logic, in that it takes an hour off the total time. Your performance after skipping an hours work in the gym, for example would be greatly improved. Train hard. Fight easy. Practice the AWA.

It's an extra one hour of focus an demands the brain's immediate energy, which unfortunately isn't ready. That's exactly why thousands of students rate really poor on their last 2-3 pieces. They're just not up for more time, because their brains still feel drained. Therefore, if you don't miss the essay during your preparation, you can write in the same test conditions as on test day, preparing the brain for the major encounter.

How long should it be?

The essay graders know you only have 30 minutes to write per AWA essay and they also know you won't be able to cover every possible point, explanation, and rebuttal. Therefore, they don't want you to write a super-long thorough review of the problem or point you're given.

When looking at the ETS sample essays, the number of terms from a 5.0-graded essay to a 6.0-graded essay increases dramatically. My advice is to write around 500-600 words. Studies demonstrate that this is an optimal amount of words for scoring. After 600, your essay appears rushed and mistakes creep in. hence I suggest 500-600 as a good amount.

The most interesting thing about the GRE essay segment is that each and every essay subject that appears on the actual exam is already reported on the official ETS website. The downside is - There are nearly 200 of them! Practicing each of these subjects is not recommended, because it would take a lot of time and energy and there is no point as you would need to take too much time away from the other sections. I have some real life examples of the essay questions later on in this book; take a look through them to get an idea of the questions you could be asked.

Currently, most subjects on the GRE Essay site can be loosely divided into five groups. I made it simple for you and listed the five categories below...

Government

Education

Arts

Politics

Economics

Sciences and Technology

So when you practice writing an essay, make sure you submit at least one essay from each of these groups.

The dissertation questions are composed of cryptic words, and often impossible to comprehend. As the essay topics are included in here, give them a look-over, spot all the words that you don't know when reading. Learning these new words will mean that you understand the subject well or at least give you a very good chance.

How to grade your essays?

The marking criteria to use are here:

Scores 6 and 5.5

Sustains insightful, in-depth analysis of complex ideas; develops and supports main points with logically compelling reasons and/or highly persuasive examples; is well focused and well organized; skilfully uses sentence variety and precise vocabulary to convey meaning effectively; demonstrates superior facility with sentence structure and language usage, but may have minor errors that do not interfere with meaning.

Scores 5 and 4.5

Provides generally thoughtful analysis of complex ideas; develops and supports main points with logically sound reasons and/or well-chosen examples; is generally focused and well organized; uses sentence variety and vocabulary to convey meaning clearly; demonstrates good control of sentence structure and language usage, but may have minor errors that do not interfere with meaning.

Scores 4 and 3.5

Provides competent analysis of ideas; develops and supports main points with relevant reasons and/or examples; is adequately organized; conveys meaning with reasonable clarity; demonstrates satisfactory control of sentence structure and language usage, but may have some errors that affect clarity.

Scores 3 and 2.5

Displays some competence in analytical writing, although the writing is flawed in at least one of the following ways: limited analysis or development; weak organization; weak control of sentence structure or language usage, with errors that often result in vagueness or lack of clarity.

Scores 2 and 1.5

Displays serious weaknesses in analytical writing. The writing is seriously flawed in at least one of the following ways: serious lack of analysis or development; lack of organization; serious and frequent problems in sentence structure or language usage, with errors that obscure meaning.

Scores 1 and 0.5

Displays fundamental deficiencies in analytical writing. The writing is fundamentally flawed in at least one of the following ways: content that is extremely confusing or mostly irrelevant to the assigned tasks; little or no development; severe and pervasive errors that result in incoherence.

Score Level 0

The examinee's analytical writing skills cannot be evaluated because the responses do not address any part of the assigned tasks, are merely attempts to copy the assignments, are in a foreign language or display only indecipherable text.

Score NS

The examinee produced no text whatsoever.

In order to score your work, try and get somebody to help you, Buddies, Relatives, and Experts even. However amazing it may seem, sometimes your buddies will help you get better results. They will help you find the errors you haven't made clear yet, and you even get an outsider's perspective on your papers, and therefore your opinions. So, even though your mates may be untrained or ignorant of the GRE AWA rating system, the opportunity to have a second pair of eyes look at your work may be very useful in discovering your shortcomings. Oh, you get reviews right on your own time frame, and sometimes it's the easiest way to think.

But before you let your friends or family assess your papers, you should remind them that you had just 30 minutes to compose your essay, and they shouldn't expect you to submit award-winning work. You should also advise them to pay attention and then decide on the following aspects of your essay: composition, logical flow of thoughts, and illustration persuasiveness. Ideally, you shouldn't try amazing vocabulary or sentence structure.

However, if you're too embarrassed to ask your friends or relatives, consider asking an accomplished professor at your college, preferably a linguistic professor or someone who's very good at formal, written English. Such teachers not only give you an objective evaluation of your essays, they give you useful feedback into just where you can develop your writing skills.

Self-evaluation if you don't have access to any teachers or smart buddies who can help you assess your AWA papers, you're the next best choice. Self-evaluation, while sometimes not recommended, can be a very helpful option for you. There are hundreds of mock essays on the internet and you can reach different GRE essays with quick google.

If you can equate your answers to others on the internet, you can guess approximately whether your answer is similar to the 4.0 or 5.0 ranges. If you can do this enough times, you'll start seeing a definite trend that will help you predict your average AWA ranking.

This sounds very complicated, and it's a rather challenging and time-consuming method, which is why you should try to take this solution as a last measure; if you can't consider any other helpful enough.

If you're an internet nerd, you'd definitely accept that sometimes internet strangers are very helpful in general. There are a number of GRE forums which are very helpful.

Issue Essay vs Argument Essay:

The GRE's Analytical Writing Assessment (AWA) section requires you to complete two different but complementary written tasks: Issue Essay and Argument Essay. Each assignment tests your writing, including testing your critical thinking. Each of these essay questions was allotted 30 minutes each, scored on a 6.0 scale.

I find that so many of the mistakes made in this section are due to the confusions of these two types of task. You need different approaches to address each of the question types. We will go deep into both of these essay questions you can see on the GRE, but for now note that the GRE Question Essay needs you to create and defend your views on a specific 'problem' that has been presented to you, while the GRE Argument Essay needs you to verify the validity or the logical consistency of an statement that has been built by another person without requiring yourself to see the difference.

Issue vs Argument:

1. Your Opinion vs. Their Opinion: The GRE Topic Essay essentially checks your ability to disagree with your opinions, and your willingness to convince people to agree with your opinions. As you can easily see here, you can give your own opinions and add important points to your answer to persuade the reader to agree. The GRE Argument Essay however needs you to evaluate a brief statement written by another author, objectively refute the claim or the author's point of view, offer ample proof and raise reasonable questions.

2. Generic vs. Specific the debatable subject offered to you for research is very general

any area. Therefore, you do not normally need a very deep knowledge of the subject. The problem is clearly presented as a statement, and your task is to choose a hand, stick to it until the end without fiddling about, and present your viewpoints, analysis, and final conclusions in a fitting manner.

However, the speaker himself makes a statement with his / her supporting proof in the form of a paragraph of a Claim article. The task is to see how rational the claim is to test if this statement is true or not, whether the argument was made on strong grounds, with adequate proof or not. Then actively refute the claim by taking sides. If you want to substantiate the author's point of view, you should cite your own facts to validate the arguments, and if you choose to go against the point of view, then you will be able to ask detailed questions and test the authenticity of the proof of the case.

3. Analysis vs. Reasoning: the solutions to the issue and argument essays also vary. The instructions given for an Argument Essay read something like this: "Write a comment to explore the argument's specified and/or unstated assumptions. Make sure to explain if the statement relies on the assumptions and what the consequences are if the theories are unwarranted. "Or like this: discuss if effective you consider this claim. Be sure to evaluate the line of logic and the application of proof in the claim. You might need to remember, for example, what problematic conclusions underlie reasoning and what alternate theories or counterexamples may undermine the inference. You may also address what sort of facts would support or contradict the claim, what adjustments would make it more scientifically valid, and what, if anything, would help you properly determine the conclusion.

And the directions given for an Issue Essay are completely different from the Argument Essay, because unlike the Argument Essay, the Issue Essay may be followed by a varying collection of guidelines, and there is no guide to follow. For starters, at the end of your test day, you may see either of the following directions:

Write a letter to clarify the degree to which you accept or disagree with the argument and describe the rationale for your stance. When forming and defending your argument, consider whether the assertion may or might not be valid and clarify how these assumptions form your opinion.

Write a letter to address the degree to which you accept or disagree with the suggestion and clarify the rationale for your decision. Describe particular conditions under which following the advice would or would not be beneficial and clarify how such situations form the situation.

Write a comment to address the degree to which you agree or disagree. When establishing and defending your stance, make sure to answer the most persuasive arguments and/or facts to contradict your opinion.

Write a comment to address which perspective aligns more favourably with your own viewpoint and clarify the rationale for your stance. When establishing and defending your argument, all viewpoints will be discussed.

Write a letter to address the degree to which you support or disagree with the assertion and the justification for the dispute.

Write a letter to clarify your policy positions and explain the rationale for your stance. When designing and defending your strategy, consider the potential implications of enforcing the policy and clarify how these results influence your stance.

4. 4.In an Issue Essay, note that you must be able to quickly present the problem at hand in your own language, using your own conclusion, while in an Argument Essay, the argument presented must be addressed from the author's point of view using their own conclusion. There is such a major contrast between the two papers, and often students choose to do the reverse more often than not, and they end up with mediocre grades. You should also be transparent about whose conclusion you consider: yours, or the writer.

5. Reasons vs. Flaws: In the second paragraph is where you can mention the side you have selected and the reasons for standing by it. Whereas in an Issue Essay, the second sentence starts with the main mistake found in the author's statement. Often, address whether the author's argument overlooks this big error.

6. True Examples vs. Fictional Examples: The content of the text will certainly contain specific true-world facts justifying the argument. Note, not only must the examples you give be important, but they must be actual, accurate examples. You can't build proofs from thin air on your own. But in an Argument article, you have the freedom to build your own explanations as long as they are applicable to the subject and as long as they adequately substantiate the point you are trying to make.

7. Appreciating vs. Questioning: Issue Essay's thesis argument often includes agreeing with the opposite perspective of one or two sentences. While you do not want to side with the opposite perspective, you will note that it might be correct in a few cases, too. You will do so to prove your moral intelligence. However, in an Argument article, the thesis arguments conclude with a note of scepticism, where you argue

that the reasoning may have one or two legitimate points but are otherwise entirely faulty.

8. Agreement vs. Disagreement: Agreeing to the point of view offered in the Issue Essay gives you more reasons to write, because more often than not, the subject posed to you is a general problem, and there will be few reasons to criticize, whilst there will be lots of points to support the argument in the question.

Yet in the Argument Essay, the situation is completely different. The statement given is intentionally designed to appear pessimistic, and because the argument given involves a logical review of the arguments raised rather than your own opinions, you should and will go against the author's opinion. Because the author's point of view will be skewed more times than not, you'll have plenty of arguments to make, so it's easier for you to criticize the author's claim instead of attempting to defend it.

9. Limitation vs. Liberty: A very critical thing to note is that you can simply show that the proof justifying the argument is incorrect, not that the argument itself is false. The conclusion is usually right, but you may doubt or challenge the validity of the statement, meaning, ask how the author came to such a statement without appropriate statements. But it's never prudent to suggest the hypothesis itself is false, so you need to limit yourself to suggesting the argument needs more proof. Within an issue argument however you can use and justify your point. Since the subject is so general in nature, you can use some facts to justify your argument, even though they suggest the conclusion is false.

10. Statement vs. Proof: The Issue Essay relies on actual, reliable data, because there is no truth in the topic. The problem is a plain, abstract argument, and no proof would be given. That's why you should look out your own facts and determine whether to accept or doubt the author's argument. But the Claim Article also contains its own proof inside the articles to be examined and attacked.

11. 11. Two Sides vs. One Claim: The Issue Essay is often like a two-sided coin, framed as a controversial two-sided subject, where you have the choice to go with the side you can best portray. However, Argument Essay has no two sides to pick from. It has one statement to be analyzed.

One of the things that daunt GRE test takers is essay writing: specifically, the fear of being tested on a topic or concept they may have no idea or knowledge about. Don't worry about this, as the GRE tests your ability to write an essay on general knowledge content, think back to all those family dinners, and your father arguing how mobile phones are destroying creativity and intelligence, or your uncle claiming that higher education should be free for all, and you'll know exactly what I mean, these are the topics that the GRE wants you talk about, just with a greater degree of sophistication.

I have also included below a few example essays, so you can use the information I have given you, and the strategies to get an amazing score on your AWA

GRE ISSUE Essay

"Colleges should require students to engage in public-service activities in order to assure that each student receives a balanced, well-rounded education."

An example answer to this is below:

Education is not just imparting academic knowledge amongst students. It is the development of all around personality of a student in order to make him eligible to adjust and succeed in the society. That is why along with cognitive development, education should seek physical, cultural, moral and social development of the child. I agree with the statement that engaging students in public-service activities helps in their all-around development. I would like to add that this should be an extension to curriculum followed in schools for children's social development.

Moreover, along with engaging students in public-service activities, it is important to inculcate values like helpfulness, social responsibility and respect towards every work, even if it is small, so that they do not view any task as a menial job, and have the willingness to continue doing it in their later lives. Each individual is a member of the society. Therefore, it is important that students are educated about their role in the society. Every citizen of the society has a social responsibility. They need to realize their responsibility at the right time so that they perform their duties well. College is the pinnacle of students' education. It is here that they are finally prepared to face the world and be at their own. Hence, the curriculum of colleges should not only include the academic part, but must also concentrate on social education. If the students are made to do works like cleaning a public park, extending help to patients like donating blood and helping poor to get food, medicines etc., it will develop a feeling of compassion amongst them for the needy and also make them realize their role as a responsible citizen.

It is often seen that the young misuse public utilities like water. Many times public taps are kept running and leaking. No one makes an effort to close these taps and save water. It is only when the students are made to do public services that they realize the importance of such things.

Therefore, if colleges step-in and encourage the students to avoid wasting water, and provide clean drinking water to the needy, it will help in building up good values and guidelines for them. This will encourage them to follow these guidelines throughout their lives. As I have mentioned earlier, it is not only the colleges that should keep in mind the all-around development of a student, but the schools should also ensure that they form the basis for the same. Therefore, the curriculum in a school should also include social education where students should be taught the benefits of maintaining good social behaviour. It is only when our educational institutions help in inculcating such habits that we can have a healthy society of balanced individuals. Such a step from the colleges and schools encourages the students to take up the cause of social work and eradicate evils from the society.

It is true that each individual cannot become a social worker, or is not able to join a social service institute, but we can do our little bit by following the path taught in colleges. Respecting the importance of public property and engaging in a little social work makes a person more conscientious and dutiful towards the society. These values surely go a long way in developing a balanced and all around personality of a person.

Below I have some example issue topics. These are examples, think about the way that they're graded, plan your time, and get somebody to score them for you!

Issue topics that could come up, there are some examples below of the type of issue essay prompts that you could expect on the day, read them and notice similarities and differences, and then when you're ready, start answering some.

Important truths begin as outrageous, or at least uncomfortable, attacks upon the accepted wisdom of the time.

Write a response in which you discuss the extent to which you agree or disagree with the claim. In developing and supporting your position, be sure to address the most compelling reasons and/or examples that could be used to challenge your position.

Use the space below to plan your essay, and write your essay on lined paper. File your essays, and look back through your plans to assess your progress as you get used to the format of the essays

Originality does not mean thinking something that was never thought before, it means putting old ideas together in new ways....

Write a response in which you discuss the extent to which you agree or disagree with the claim. In developing and supporting your position, be sure to address the most compelling reasons and/or examples that could be used to challenge your position.

Use the space below to plan your essay, and write your essay on lined paper. File your essays, and look back through your plans to assess your progress as you get used to the format of the essays

Laws should not be rigid or fixed. Instead, they should be flexible enough to take account of various circumstances, times, and places.

Write a response in which you discuss the extent to which you agree or disagree with the claim. In developing and supporting your position, be sure to address the most compelling reasons and/or examples that could be used to challenge your position.

Use the space below to plan your essay, and write your essay on lined paper. File your essays, and look back through your plans to assess your progress as you get used to the format of the essays

It is always an individual who is the impetus for innovation the details may be worked out by a team, but true innovation results from the enterprise and unique perception of an individual....

Write a response in which you discuss the extent to which you agree or disagree with the claim. In developing and supporting your position, be sure to address the most compelling reasons and/or examples that could be used to challenge your position.

Use the space below to plan your essay, and write your essay on lined paper. File your essays, and look back through your plans to assess your progress as you get used to the format of the essays

The function of science is to reassure; the purpose of art is to upset.

Write a response in which you discuss the extent to which you agree or disagree with the claim. In developing and supporting your position, be sure to address the most compelling reasons and/or examples that could be used to challenge your position.

Use the space below to plan your essay, and write your essay on lined paper. File your essays, and look back through your plans to assess your progress as you get used to the format of the essays

It is possible to pass laws that control or place limits on people's behaviour, but legislation cannot reform human nature.

Write a response in which you discuss the extent to which you agree or disagree with the claim. In developing and supporting your position, be sure to address the most compelling reasons and/or examples that could be used to challenge your position.

Use the space below to plan your essay, and write your essay on lined paper. File your essays, and look back through your plans to assess your progress as you get used to the format of the essays

Laws cannot change what is in people's hearts and minds....

Write a response in which you discuss the extent to which you agree or disagree with the claim. In developing and supporting your position, be sure to address the most compelling reasons and/or examples that could be used to challenge your position.

Use the space below to plan your essay, and write your essay on lined paper. File your essays, and look back through your plans to assess your progress as you get used to the format of the essays

What most human beings really want to attain is not knowledge, but certainty. Gaining real knowledge requires taking risks and keeping the mind open.

Write a response in which you discuss the extent to which you agree or disagree with the claim. In developing and supporting your position, be sure to address the most compelling reasons and/or examples that could be used to challenge your position.

Use the space below to plan your essay, and write your essay on lined paper. File your essays, and look back through your plans to assess your progress as you get used to the format of the essays

Many problems of modern society cannot be solved by laws and the legal system because moral behaviour cannot be legislated.

Write a response in which you discuss the extent to which you agree or disagree with the claim. In developing and supporting your position, be sure to address the most compelling reasons and/or examples that could be used to challenge your position.

Use the space below to plan your essay, and write your essay on lined paper. File your essays, and look back through your plans to assess your progress as you get used to the format of the essays

The way students and scholars interpret the materials they work with in their academic fields is more a matter of personality than of training.

Write a response in which you discuss the extent to which you agree or disagree with the claim. In developing and supporting your position, be sure to address the most compelling reasons and/or examples that could be used to challenge your position.

Use the space below to plan your essay, and write your essay on lined paper. File your essays, and look back through your plans to assess your progress as you get used to the format of the essays

Governments should place few if any, restrictions on scientific research and development.

Write a response in which you discuss the extent to which you agree or disagree with the recommendation and explain your reasoning for the position you take. In developing and supporting your position, describe specific circumstances in which adopting the recommendation would or would not be advantageous and explain how these examples shape your position.

Use the space below to plan your essay, and write your essay on lined paper. File your essays, and look back through your plans to assess your progress as you get used to the format of the essays

Claim: It is no longer possible for a society to regard any living man or woman as a hero.

Reason: The reputation of anyone who is subjected to media scrutiny will eventually be diminished.

Write a response in which you discuss the extent to which you agree or disagree with the claim and the reason on which that claims is based.

Use the space below to plan your essay, and write your essay on lined paper. File your essays, and look back through your plans to assess your progress as you get used to the format of the essays

College students should base their choice of a field of study on the availability of jobs in that field.

Write a response in which you discuss the extent to which you agree or disagree with the claim. In developing and supporting your position, be sure to address the most compelling reasons and/or examples that could be used to challenge your position.

Use the space below to plan your essay, and write your essay on lined paper. File your essays, and look back through your plans to assess your progress as you get used to the format of the essays

Young people should be encouraged to pursue long-term, realistic goals rather than seek immediate fame and recognition.

Write a response in which you discuss the extent to which you agree or disagree with the statement and explain your reasoning for the position you take. In developing and supporting your position, you should consider ways in which the statement might or might not hold true and explain how these considerations shape your position.

Use the space below to plan your essay, and write your essay on lined paper. File your essays, and look back through your plans to assess your progress as you get used to the format of the essays

Well, there you have it! You now have a general idea of what kind of questions you could expect in the issue task, and the structure of the issue prompts. As you can see, these are questions of a sweeping, unspecified nature, and usually, students find their own experiences, opinions, and awareness sufficient to write a satisfactory essay. Topics like education, healthcare, R&D, art, politics, social media and gender are usually hot favorites for the ETS, so reading up on these areas and writing a few practice essays can prove to be immensely helpful.

Argument topic examples and essays

As discussed earlier, The GRE Argument writing task is designed to test your ability to your critical-reasoning and analytic (as well as writing) skills. Your task is to compose an essay in which you provide a focused critique of the stated argument — but not to present your own views on the argument's topic.

The following GRE-style Argument prompt consists of an argument followed by a directive for responding to the argument. Keep in mind: the argument itself is not from the official pool, and so you won't see this one on the actual GRE.

GRE Argument Prompt

The following appeared in the editorial column of the Fern County Gazette newspaper:

"The Fern County Council made the right decision when it unanimously voted to convert the Northside branch of the county library system into a computer-skills training facility for public use. The converted facility will fill what is certain, based on national trends, to be a growing need among county residents for training in computer skills. And since our library system boasts more volumes per resident than any other system in the state, the remaining branches will adequately serve the future needs of Fern County residents."

Discuss what evidence you would need to properly evaluate the argument, and explain how that evidence might strengthen or weaken the argument.

Following is a sample essay that responds to the above prompt. As you read the essay, keep in mind:

Each of the three body paragraphs identifies a different aspect of the argument, discusses what additional evidence is needed to properly evaluate that aspect, and explains how that evidence might bear on the argument.

This essay is brief enough to plan and type in 30 minutes.

The essay is intended as a benchmark response — one that would earn a top score of 6. But it is by no means "the" correct response to the prompt. Other top-scoring essays might be organized differently or provide supporting examples that are different than the ones given here.

Sample Argument Essay (490 Words)

This editorial argues that the Fern County Council's decision to convert a library branch to a computer-skills training facility was the "right" one. However, its author fails to provide sufficient information to permit a proper evaluation of the argument's reasoning. Each point of deficiency is discussed separately below.

One of the argument's deficiencies involves the claim, based on a national trend, that there is "certain" to be a growing need in Fern County for computer-skills training. The author provides no specific evidence that the county conforms to the cited trend. Lacking such evidence, it is entirely possible that the Fern County residents are, by and large, already highly proficient in using computers. Of course, it is also possible that a large and growing segment of the local population consists of senior citizens and/or young children — two groups who typically need computer-skills training — or unemployed workers needing to learn computer skills in order to find jobs. In any event, more information about the county's current and anticipated demographics is needed in order to determine the extent to which Fern County residents actually need and would use the Northside computer-training facility.

Another of the argument's deficiencies is that it provides no information about alternative means of providing computer-skills training to county residents. Perhaps certain local businesses or schools already provide computer-training facilities and services to the general public — in which case it would be useful to know whether those alternatives are affordable for most county residents and whether they suffice to meet anticipated demand. Or perhaps county residents are for the most part willing to teach themselves computer skills at home using books, DVDs and online tutorials — in which case it would be helpful to know the extent to which affordable broadband Internet access is available to Fern County households. If it turns out that county residents can easily obtain computer-skills training through means such as these, converting the Northside branch might not have been a sensible idea.

Yet another of the editorial's shortcomings has to do with the number of books in the Fern County library system. The mere fact that the system boasts a great number of books per capita does not necessarily mean that the supply is adequate or that it will be adequate in the future. A full assessment of whether the remaining branches provide adequate shelf space and/or printed materials would require detailed information about the library system's inventory vis-à-vis the current and anticipated needs and interests of Fern County residents. If more, or more types, of printed books and periodicals are needed, then it would appear in retrospect that converting the Northside branch to a computer training center was a bad idea.

In a nutshell, then, a proper evaluation of the editorial requires more information about current as well as anticipated demand for computer-skills training in Fern County and about the adequacy of the library system's stacks to meet the interests and preferences of the county's residents.

Following is a sample essay that responds to the above prompt. As you read the essay, keep in mind:

Each of the three body paragraphs identifies a different aspect of the argument, discusses what additional evidence is needed to properly evaluate that aspect, and explains how that evidence might bear on the argument.

This essay is brief enough to plan and type in 30 minutes.

The essay is intended as a benchmark response — one that would earn a top score of 6. But it is by no means "the" correct response to the prompt. Other top-scoring essays might be organized differently or provide supporting examples that are different than the ones given here.

Take a look at the key features and when you attempt your essays, try and use the same structure in the planning section.

Argument:

The following appeared in a memo from a vice president of Alta Manufacturing.

"During the past year, Alta Manufacturing had thirty percent more on-the-job accidents than nearby Zanzibar Inc., where the work shifts are one hour shorter than ours. Experts believe that a significant contributing factor in many on-the-job accidents is fatigue and sleep deprivation among workers. Therefore, to reduce the number of on-the-job accidents at Alta and thereby increase productivity, we should shorten each of our three work shifts by one hour so that our employees will get adequate amounts of sleep."

Essay

The given argument presents a couple of assumptions to arrive at the conclusion that shortening the work shifts by one hour will ensure that the employees of Alta Manufacturing get adequate amounts of sleep, thereby reducing the number of on-the-job accidents which in turn will increase productivity. The argument has cited the example of the Zanzibar Inc. in support of its claim that on-the-job accidents can be largely reduced by shortening the duration of the work shifts. A careful analysis of the given argument brings into focus some aspects that have been ignored while framing the argument leading to a conclusion that sounds unconvincing. Let us now discuss each of these aspects individually.

Firstly, a major flaw in the argument is that there is absolutely no direct relation between getting adequate amounts of sleep and reducing the work shifts by an hour each. The company can by no means ensure that this extra hour given to the workers will be utilized by them for sleeping. They are on their own after their work shift is over and they may utilize the additional time at hand as per their convenience. Therefore, the presumption that reducing the work shifts by an hour will ensure that workers get adequate amounts of sleep is totally baseless and unsound.

Secondly, lack of sleep may not be the primary reason for on-the-job accidents. The argument presents the example of Zanzibar Inc. where such accidents are lesser in number and cites shorter shift duration as the reason behind this. This assumption appears to be completely illogical as there can be various other factors for a lesser number of on-the-job accidents in Zanzibar Inc.. Such accidents may be attributed to the quality and condition of machines being utilized at Alta Manufacturing as compared to the ones at Zanzibar Inc. In addition, the work environment, experience of workers, usage of protective gear and the level of danger involved while working with machines are important factors to be considered while comparing the statistics of these two companies with respect to the frequency of on-the-job accidents. Therefore, attributing such accidents to fatigue and sleep deprivation in a major way seems far-fetched and illogical.

Thirdly, indicating an increase in productively as a direct outcome of lesser on-the-job accidents is, by and large, an extremely flawed assumption. It is a well-known fact that the productivity of an industry depends on efficient management, good supply chain, profitability, availability of raw materials, availability of trained/skilled manpower, efficiency of the process of production, quality and types of machines, size of the company and various other socio-economic factors. Therefore, the assumption that a reduced number of working hours and lesser on-the-job accidents will directly increase productivity has weakened the given argument. The argument lacks substantial evidence that can prove a direct link between productivity and on-the-job accidents. At the same time, one cannot ignore the fact that reducing the number of working hours may probably affect the productivity of Alta Manufacturing in a negative manner.

The given argument may have been strengthened had more evidence been included in the form of comparisons between the working conditions, quality of machines and other statistics of Alta Manufacturing and Zanzibar Inc. In its present form, due to lack of adequate evidence, the argument fails to convince the reader that the conclusion is justified.

Example Argument questions,

Below is a non-exhaustive list of examples for the argument essay, as with the issue essay, try them and get them graded?

A company called wet weather investments specialize in providing major investment advice to customers. On a recent blog post they: wrote "Homes in the North USA, where winters are typically cold, have traditionally used oil as their major fuel for heating. Last year that region experienced thirty days with below-average temperatures, and local weather forecasters throughout the region predict that this weather pattern will continue for several more years. Furthermore, many new homes have been built in this region during the past year. Because of these developments, we predict an increased demand for heating oil and recommend major investment in Mega Oil Inc. one of whose major business operations is the retail sale of home heating oil."

Write a response in which you discuss what specific evidence is needed to evaluate the argument and explain how the evidence would weaken or strengthen the argument.

Use the space below to plan your essay, and write your essay on lined paper. File your essays, and look back through your plans to assess your progress as you get used to the format of the essays

On a website of 93.6 ZAS FM radio station, the owner wrote. "To reverse a decline in listener numbers, our owners have decided that 93.6 ZAS FM must change from its current jazz-music format. The decline has occurred despite population growth in our listening area, but that growth has resulted mainly from people moving here after their retirement. We must make listeners of these new residents. We could switch to a music format tailored to their tastes, but a continuing decline in local sales of recorded music suggests limited interest in music. Instead we should change to a news and talk format, a form of radio that is increasingly popular in our area."

Write a response in which you discuss what specific evidence is needed to evaluate the argument and explain how the evidence would weaken or strengthen the argument.

Use the space below to plan your essay, and write your essay on lined paper. File your essays, and look back through your plans to assess your progress as you get used to the format of the essays

Three years ago, because of flooding at the Western Palean Wildlife Preserve, 100 lions and 100 western gazelles were moved to the East Palean Preserve, an area that is home to most of the same species that are found in the western preserve, though in larger numbers, and to the eastern gazelle, a close relative of the western gazelle. The only difference in climate is that the eastern preserve typically has slightly less rainfall. Unfortunately, after three years in the eastern preserve, the imported western gazelle population has been virtually eliminated. Since the slight reduction in rainfall cannot be the cause of the virtual elimination of western gazelle, their disappearance must have been caused by the larger number of predators in the eastern preserve.

Write a response in which you discuss what specific evidence is needed to evaluate the argument and explain how the evidence would weaken or strengthen the argument.

Use the space below to plan your essay, and write your essay on lined paper. File your essays, and look back through your plans to assess your progress as you get used to the format of the essays

The following appeared in a recommendation from the president of Milang. "In November the city of Pisal installed CCTV in its shopping district, and vandalism there declined within a month. The city of Milang has recently begun police patrols on bicycles in its shopping, but the rate of vandalism there remains constant. We should install CCTV throughout Milang, then, because doing so is a more effective way to combat crime. By reducing crime in this way, we can improve all areas of our city."

Write a response in which you discuss what specific evidence is needed to evaluate the argument and explain how the evidence would weaken or strengthen the argument.

Use the space below to plan your essay, and write your essay on lined paper. File your essays, and look back through your plans to assess your progress as you get used to the format of the essays

The following appeared in a memo from the vice president of ACME Manufacturing. "During the past year, workers at ACME Manufacturing reported 30 percent more on-the-job accidents than workers at nearby Zanzibar Inc., where the work shifts are one hour shorter than ours. A recent government study reports that fatigue and sleep deprivation among workers are significant contributing factors in many on-the-job accidents. If we shorten each of our work shifts by one hour, we can improve ACME Manufacturing's safety record by ensuring that our employees are adequately rested."

Write a response in which you discuss what specific evidence is needed to evaluate the argument and explain how the evidence would weaken or strengthen the argument.

Use the space below to plan your essay, and write your essay on lined paper. File your essays, and look back through your plans to assess your progress as you get used to the format of the essays

The following appeared in a letter to the editor of Gotham City's local newspaper. "In our region of Trillura, the majority of money spent on the schools that most students attend – the city-run public schools – comes from taxes that each city government collects. The region's cities differ, however, in the budgetary priority they give to public education. For example, both as a proportion of its overall tax revenues and in absolute terms, Gotham City has recently spent almost twice as much per year as Springstein Township has for its public schools – even though both cities have about the same number of residents. Clearly, Gotham City residents place a higher value on providing a good education in public schools than Springstein Township residents do."

Write a response in which you discuss what specific evidence is needed to evaluate the argument and explain how the evidence would weaken or strengthen the argument.

Use the space below to plan your essay, and write your essay on lined paper. File your essays, and look back through your plans to assess your progress as you get used to the format of the essays

Milk and dairy products are rich in vitamin D and calcium — substances essential for building and maintaining bones. Many people therefore say that a diet rich in dairy products can help prevent osteoporosis, a disease that is linked to both environmental and genetic factors and that causes the bones to weaken significantly with age. But a long-term study of a large number of people found that those who consistently consumed dairy products throughout the years of the study have a higher rate of bone fractures than any other participants in the study. Since bone fractures are symptomatic of osteoporosis, this study result shows that a diet rich in dairy products may actually increase, rather than decrease, the risk of osteoporosis.

Write a response in which you discuss what specific evidence is needed to evaluate the argument and explain how the evidence would weaken or strengthen the argument.

Use the space below to plan your essay, and write your essay on lined paper. File your essays, and look back through your plans to assess your progress as you get used to the format of the essays

The following appeared in a memo at WAYNE MANUFACTURING Company. "When WAYNE MANUFACTURING lies off employees, it pays Bruce's recruitment to offer those employees assistance in creating resumes and developing interviewing skills, if they so desire. Laid-off employees have benefited greatly from Bruce's recruitment's services: last year those who used Bruce's recruitment found jobs much more quickly than did those who did not. Recently, it has been proposed that we use the less expensive Joker Personnel Firm in place of Bruce's recruitment. This would be a mistake because eight years ago, when WAYNE MANUFACTURING was using Joker, only half of the workers we laid off at that time found jobs within a year. Moreover, Bruce's recruitment is clearly superior, as evidenced by its bigger staff and larger number of branch offices. After all, last year Bruce's recruitment's clients took an average of six months to find jobs, whereas Joker's clients took nine."

Write a response in which you discuss what specific evidence is needed to evaluate the argument and explain how the evidence would weaken or strengthen the argument.

Use the space below to plan your essay, and write your essay on lined paper. File your essays, and look back through your plans to assess your progress as you get used to the format of the essays

An ancient, traditional remedy for insomnia – the scent of Hop flowers – has now been proved effective. In a recent study, 30 volunteers with chronic insomnia slept each night for three weeks on Hop-scented pillows in a controlled room where their sleep was monitored electronically. During the first week, volunteers continued to take their usual sleeping medication. They slept soundly but wakened feeling tired. At the beginning of the second week, the volunteers discontinued their sleeping medication. During that week, they slept less soundly than the previous week and felt even more tired. During the third week, the volunteers slept longer and more soundly than in the previous two weeks. Therefore, the study proves that Hop cures insomnia within a short period of time.

Write a response in which you discuss what specific evidence is needed to evaluate the argument and explain how the evidence would weaken or strengthen the argument.

Use the space below to plan your essay, and write your essay on lined paper. File your essays, and look back through your plans to assess your progress as you get used to the format of the essays

Super Health R us, a chain of stores selling health food and other health-related products, is opening its next franchise in the town of Burgerton. The store should prove to be very successful: Super Health R us franchises tend to be most profitable in areas where residents lead healthy lives, and clearly Burgerton is such an area. Burgerton merchants report that sales of running shoes and exercise clothing are at all-time highs. The local health club has more members than ever, and the weight training and aerobics classes are always full. Finally, Burgerton's schoolchildren represent a new generation of potential customers: these schoolchildren are required to participate in a fitness-for-life program, which emphasizes the benefits of regular exercise at an early age.

Write a response in which you discuss what specific evidence is needed to evaluate the argument and explain how the evidence would weaken or strengthen the argument.

Use the space below to plan your essay, and write your essay on lined paper. File your essays, and look back through your plans to assess your progress as you get used to the format of the essays

The following was written as a part of an application for a small-business loan by a group of developers in the city of Denston.

"Rock music is extremely popular in the city of Denston: over 100,000 people attended Denston's annual Rock festival last summer, and the highest-rated radio program in Denston is 'Rock Nightly,' which airs every weeknight. Also, a number of well-known Rock musicians own homes in Denston. Nevertheless, the nearest Rock club is over an hour away. Given the popularity of Rock in Denston and a recent nationwide study indicating that the typical Rock fan spends close to $1,000 per year on Rock entertainment, a Rock music club in Denston would be tremendously profitable."

Write a response in which you examine the stated and/or unstated assumptions of the argument. Be sure to explain how the argument depends on these assumptions, and what the implications are for the argument if the assumptions prove unwarranted.

Use the space below to plan your essay, and write your essay on lined paper. File your essays, and look back through your plans to assess your progress as you get used to the format of the essays

The following appeared in a letter to the editor of a journal on environmental issues. "Over the past year, the Gold Digging Inc. (GDI) has purchased over 10,000 square miles of land in the tropical nation of East Lanarkshire. Mining copper on this land will inevitably result in pollution and, since East Lanarkshire is the home of several endangered animal species, in environmental disaster. But such disasters can be prevented if consumers simply refuse to purchase products that are made with GDI's copper unless the company abandons its mining plans."

Write a response in which you examine the stated and/or unstated assumptions of the argument. Be sure to explain how the argument depends on these assumptions, and what the implications are for the argument if the assumptions prove unwarranted.

Use the space below to plan your essay, and write your essay on lined paper. File your essays, and look back through your plans to assess your progress as you get used to the format of the essays

The following appeared in a memo from the vice president of marketing at Super Glove, Inc. "A recent study of our customers suggests that our company is wasting the money it spends on its patented Endure manufacturing process, which ensures that our Gloves are strong enough to last for two years. We have always advertised our use of the Endure process, but the new study shows that despite our Gloves' durability, our average customer actually purchases new Super Gloves every three months. Furthermore, our customers surveyed in our largest market, northeastern United States cities, say that they most value Super Gloves' stylish appearance and availability in many colors. These findings suggest that we can increase our profits by discontinuing use of the Endure manufacturing process."

Write a response in which you examine the stated and/or unstated assumptions of the argument. Be sure to explain how the argument depends on these assumptions, and what the implications are for the argument if the assumptions prove unwarranted.

Use the space below to plan your essay, and write your essay on lined paper. File your essays, and look back through your plans to assess your progress as you get used to the format of the essays

While the Department of Education in the state of Attra recommends that high school students be assigned homework every day, the data from a recent statewide survey of high school math and science teachers give us reason to question the usefulness of daily homework. In the district of Sanlee, 86 percent of the teachers reported assigning homework three to five times a week, whereas in the district of Marlee, less than 25 percent of the teachers reported assigning homework three to five times a week. Yet the students in Marlee earn better grades overall and are less likely to be required to repeat a year of school than are the students in Sanlee. Therefore, all teachers in our high schools should assign homework no more than twice a week.

Write a response in which you examine the stated and/or unstated assumptions of the argument. Be sure to explain how the argument depends on these assumptions, and what the implications are for the argument if the assumptions prove unwarranted.

Use the space below to plan your essay, and write your essay on lined paper. File your essays, and look back through your plans to assess your progress as you get used to the format of the essays

The following is a recommendation from the personnel director to the president of Oxford Publishing Company. "Many other companies have recently stated that having their employees take the Easy Type Speed-Typing Course has greatly improved productivity. One graduate of the course was able to type a 500-page report in only two hours; another graduate rose from an assistant manager to vice president of the company in under a year. Obviously, the faster you can type, the more information you can convert in a single workday. Moreover, Easy Type would cost Oxford only $500 per employee — a small price to pay when you consider the benefits. Included in this fee is a three-week seminar in Spruce City and a lifelong subscription to the Easy Type newsletter. Clearly, Oxford would benefit greatly by requiring all of our employees to take the Easy Type course."

Write a response in which you examine the stated and/or unstated assumptions of the argument. Be sure to explain how the argument depends on these assumptions, and what the implications are for the argument if the assumptions prove unwarranted.

Use the space below to plan your essay, and write your essay on lined paper. File your essays, and look back through your plans to assess your progress as you get used to the format of the essays

How to take a practice GRE

A practice test is not just another homework assignment. It is an important opportunity for you to get as accurate a picture as possible of your readiness to earn a score that will make you proud. Your results will help you make informed decisions about your prep schedule and keep your study sessions productive.

Full timed practice tests give you an insight into areas that will be critical to your success on Test Day: did you run out of time in any of the sections?

Have you been nervous?

Have you been hungry?

Have you got thirsty?

Did you get sick of that?

Have you been able to stay focused?

Have you survived 3.5 hours of waking up without looking at your phone?

Eat a healthy dinner the night before the practice test, including slow-release energy carbohydrates (for example, rice, pasta, potatoes). It's a mental marathon— but you're supposed to fuel your body and mind as if you're running a real one.

Get a good night's sleep (at least 8 hours) Wake up no later than 7:00 a.m.— that's how it's going to be on Test Day Saturday morning, so try doing it the same way for a practice test if you can!

Eat a healthy breakfast (for example: coffee, fruit, eggs, pancakes, toast— nothing too sugary!) Be prepared Use real paper to write the sample-you'll write it by hand on Test Day!

Water and healthy snacks on hand-your kitchen won't be next to the Testing Site!

If possible, take a practice test in a library— not at home comfort No distractions!

Turn off your phone and leave it in your bag If you need to use your phone as a timer, put it in Airplane Devices On Test Day mode, you will not be allowed to access your phone or any other electronic device at all— not even during breaks — or your scores may be cancelled. Don't do that during a practice test! For these 3.5 hours, you need to know what it feels like to be disconnected.

Top tips:

Be truthful with yourself: give yourself the exact amount of time indicated for each segment. Don't allow yourself a few extra seconds to fill in the bubbles with questions you haven't been asked yet. If you do that on Test Day, your scores may be cancelled.

Here are some helpful questions to consider while evaluating your performance: did you sleep at least 8 hours

On the night before the practice test?

Have you woken up at least one hour before the practice test?

Have you eaten a healthy breakfast?

Have you been happy with your breakfast? Would you like to try another kind of breakfast food next time?

Have you started the test at 8:30am?

Did someone take the exam for you?

Have you used a written test sheet and a bubble disk?

Have you taken one sitting?

Have you allowed yourself a test day break (one 15 minute break after the third multiple-choice section)?

Did you drink any water during the breaks?

Did you eat healthy snacks during the break?

Have your snacks made you happy? Treat yourself during the break—you should only eat healthy and happy snacks!

Now I will leave you with some practical advice about the day of the exam. The best way to prepare is by practicing test questions (coming up!). Try to treat each one like a real exam. Practice the conditions of the day (as best you can) so that you are not caught out.

I have some final tips/pointers about the last things to do before and exam, below. Use these tips in your practice tests, and in the real thing. And good luck!

The 10 best study tips and tricks for the night before the exam

It's the night before the big exam. The hard work is done, your preparation has come to an end, and now is the ideal time to calm down your nerves and make sure that you're ready to enter the exam hall well rested and confident in your ability to write an outstanding exam essay.

1. Play it safe: One of the first rules to run a marathon is not to do it in new shoes. The principle of' nothing new' in sporting events applies to food, apparel, habits, and so on. If you haven't done anything in the past, it's not time to experiment with new memorization methods, pharmaceuticals (legal or illegal) or job habits. Go with what worked best in the past, no matter how much someone might try to convince you of a newer, better, or faster way. And this includes how much of the advice you might want to take.

2. Ready well in advance there's an old adage that says,' well started is half done.' Even before you spend the night before the exam is up, you should also spend the days before the night before you get dressed. The night before the test, it's not time to hunt down the book from the library that your professor insisted on reading at. Everything you need to prepare for the exam should be available for use the night before so that you can make the most of your time.

3. Sleep is a friend of yours. Most people think that the best use of their study time is to sacrifice sleep so that they can study more. Yet study after study shows that having enough rest is key to the way you process new information. I suggest this: come home and take a little nap before you continue your studies (20-30 minutes). Start fresh, then. Get a regular night's sleep for 6.5-8 hours, but go to bed early. Then start studying the first thing again when you wake up until it's times to take the exam. This will give you two opportunities to re-energize the material. If you skip to sleep, you'll never really feel fresh, and most likely you'll just feel irritable, distracted, and burned.

4. Eat right. You want to eat healthy, with a nice mixture of good carbs, proteins and fats. It might be best to avoid a massive carb that's just going to make you sleep with a sugar crash, especially on the morning of the exam. Probably the best way to avoid taking too much caffeine as well. Drink plenty of water to help the brain function optimum. You want to get the most out of your food and drink, but you don't want to use it to popular your returns.

5. One of the most effective ways to prepare for an exam is by actually taking an exam for yourself. Go through all your materials (textbooks, notes, ancillary materials) and look for questions. Suppose that you are the most cruel and sadistic interviewer to have ever existed. Then take the test. It will definitely give you an idea of where your

strengths and weaknesses lie.

6. Study groups and study buddies there is a very high chance that you are not the only one preparing for the same exam the night before. Find someone or a group of people you trust to stay on the job and want to do well and study with them. It's best to arrange this ahead of time, but this can be a very effective way to prepare for an exam. It makes the best sense, however, to keep the number small and to work with people who might be slightly more efficient than you are in class.

7. Go offline (scary but necessary) Unless there is an important, study-related reason you need to be linked to Instagram, Snapchat, TikTok, and so on, you can consider dropping the face of the virtual world for a few days. It might start with the need for Google to name something that might be on the exam and end up two hours later with you laughing at a cat video and hating how you got sucked down another rabbit hole. For the 12-24 hours leading up to the test, the only thing you need to concentrate on is the exam. Everything else could be waiting.

8. Limit distractions and contacts getting off the Internet, or just turning off your computer, is limiting your distractions. Those, sadly, could be a few. Today, of course, there are people who actually think and work better with the noise around them. But what we're talking about here is the distraction that will suck up the time needed: your housemate who wants to recount last night's antics, a friend who wants to hit the stores with you, your mom who won't stop calling... If best you can, be inaccessible until the exam is over.

9. As far as structuring your time goes, you can't do any worse than the famous Pomodoro productivity model. This method has been developed by Francesco Cirillo and is based on the little red tomato kitchen timers. Essentially, work one thing with the timer set for 20-25 minutes. Then take a short break (stretch your legs, get a drink). Then go for another 25 minutes. Take a long break for 15-30 minutes after 4-5 sets of 20-25 minutes. Then continue again. The most important part of this method is that you focus entirely on the task at hand for those 20-25 minutes. But, as always, see #1.

10. Be ready to go: The closer you get to the next day, and definitely the next morning, the more nervous you get, and potentially the more oriented you get to the test. On the day before your test, I suggest that you get everything you need in advance. Have your clothes ready to wear (and better go with layers in case the room is too warm or too cold). Have what you're going to eat more or less ready to eat. It's

probably best to have a shower the night before. This way, you won't have to make too much effort to get ready in the morning.

Go to the exam room prepared, concentrated and relaxed. Good luck, this is what you have!

Good Luck, now try these practice tests.

Section 1: Issue topic

Some people believe that corporations have a responsibility to promote the well-being of the societies and environments in which they operate. Others believe that the only responsibility of corporations, provided they operate within the law, is to make as much money as possible.

Write a response in which you discuss which view more closely aligns with your own position and explain your reasoning for the position you take. In developing and supporting your position, you should address both of the views presented.

Section 2: Argument topic

Directions:

You will be given a short passage that presents an argument, or an argument to be completed, and specific instructions on how to respond to that passage. You will have 30 minutes to plan and compose a response in which you analyze the passage according to the specific instructions. A response to any other argument will receive a score of zero.

Note that you are NOT being asked to present your own views on the subject. Make sure that you respond to the specific instructions and support your analysis with relevant reasons and/or examples.

The following appeared in an editorial in a business magazine.

"Although the sales of Whirlwind video games have declined over the past two years, a recent survey of video-game players suggests that this sales trend is about to be reversed. The survey asked video-game players what features they thought were most important in a video game. According to the survey, players prefer games that provide lifelike graphics, which require the most up-to-date computers. Whirlwind has just introduced several such games with an extensive advertising campaign directed at people ten to twenty-five years old, the age-group most likely to play video games. It follows, then, that the sales of Whirlwind video games are likely to increase dramatically in the next few months."

Write a response in which you examine the stated and/or unstated assumptions of the argument. Be sure to explain how the argument depends on these assumptions and what the implications are for the argument if the assumptions prove unwarranted.

Section 3: Quantitative reasoning

1. For each of Questions 1 to 7, compare Quantity A and Quantity B, using additional information centered above the two quantities if such information is given.

Select one of the following four answer choices and fill in the corresponding circle to the right of the question.

(A) $(-2, -3)$

(B) $(-2, 7)$

(C) (ss, tt)

(D) $(8, -3)$

2. A certain punch is created by mixing two parts soda and three parts ice cream. The soda is 4 parts sugar, 5 parts citric acid, and 11 parts other ingredients. The ice cream is 3 parts sugar, 2 parts citric acid, and 15 parts other ingredients.

Quantity A	Quantity B
Parts sugar in the punch	Parts citric acid in the punc

(A) Quantity A is greater.

(B) Quantity B is greater.

(C) The two quantities are equal.

(D) The relationship cannot be determined from the information given.

3. The average (arithmetic mean) high temperature for *x* days is 70 degrees. The addition of one day with a high temperature of 75 degrees increases the average to 71 degrees.

Quantity A	Quantity B

(A) A Quantity A is greater.

(B) B Quantity B is greater.

(C) C The two quantities are equal.

(D) D The relationship cannot be determined from the information given.

4. Each angle in triangle *QRS* has a degree measurement of either x or y and the angles are expressed by the equation $2x + y = 180$

Quantity A	Quantity B
Perimeter of *QRS*	17

(A) Quantity A is greater.

(B) Quantity B is greater.

(C) The two quantities are equal.

(D) The relationship cannot be determined from the information given.

5. The scores for the 500 students who took Ms. Johnson's final exam have a normal distribution. There are 80 students who scored at least 92 points out of a possible 100 total points and 10 students who scored at or below 56.

Quantity A	Quantity B
The average (arithmetic mean) score on the final exam	87

(A) Quantity A is greater.

(B) Quantity B is greater.

(C) The two quantities are equal.

(D) The relationship cannot be determined from the information given.

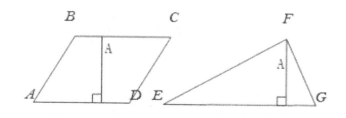

Quantity A	Quantity B
The area of *ABCD*	The area of *EFG*

(A) Quantity A is greater.

(B) Quantity B is greater.

(C) The two quantities are equal.

(D) The relationship cannot be determined from the information given.

6. $(3x - 4y)(3x + 4y) = 2$

Quantity A	Quantity B
$9x^2 - 16y^2$	4

(A) Quantity A is greater.

(B) Quantity B is greater.

(C) The two quantities are equal.

(D) The relationship cannot be determined from the information given.

8. If $8a - 2 = 22$, then $4a - 1 =$

(A) 2

(B) 11

(C) 11

(D) 12

(E) 44

9. Twenty percent of the sweaters in a store are white.

Of the remaining sweaters, 40 percent are brown, and the rest are blue. If there are 200 sweaters in the store, then how many more blue sweaters than white sweaters are in the store?

10. $\dfrac{(4^{13}-4^{12})}{4^{11}}$

(A) 0

(B) 1

(C) 4

(D) 12

(E) 16

Questions 11 through 14 refer to the following graph.

SUBSCRIPTIONS TO NEWSMAGAZINE x, 1970–1985

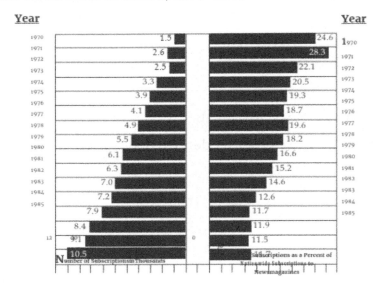

Number of Subscriptions in Thousands

Number of Subscriptions as a Percent of Nationwide Subscriptions to Newsmagazines

Note: Drawn to scale

NATIONWIDE NEWS MAGAZINE SUBSCRIPTIONS: 1972 TO 1984

Newsmagazine	1972	1975	1978	1981	1984
X	2,500	4,100	6,100	7,200	9,100
Y	1,700	3,100	4,600	5,700	7,200
Z	3,600	5,800	7,600	9,400	11,400
Others	3,500	8,900	18,500	34,700	51,300

11. What was the total number of subscriptions for Newsmagazine x during the year in which Newsmagazine x accounted for 14.6 percent of nationwide news magazine subscriptions?

(A) 1,020

(B) 1,980

(C) 6,300

(D) 7,000

(E) 7,200

12. In which of the following years did subscriptions to Newsmagazine z account for approximately $1/6$ of the total nationwide magazine subscriptions?

(A) 1984

(B) 1981

(C) 1978

(D) 1975

(E) 1972

13. What was the approximate percent increase in nationwide subscriptions to newsmagazines between 1970 and 1971 ?

(A) 4%

(B) 11%

(C) 26%

(D) 51%

(E) 73%

14. In 1973, what was the approximate number of subscriptions to newsmagazines nationwide?

(A) 3,000

(B) 13,000

(C) 16,000

(D) 20,000

(E) 67,000

15. If $a = (27)(3^{-2})$ and $x = (6)(3^{-1})$, then which of the following is equivalent to $(12)(3^{-x}) \times (15)(2^{-a})$?

(A) 5(-2245)(320)

(B) 25

(C) 52

(D) 5(24)(38)

(E) 5(2245)(320)

16. Jill has received 8 of her 12 evaluation scores. So far, Jill's average (arithmetic mean) is 3.75 out of a possible 5. If Jill needs an average of 4.0 points to get a promotion, which list of scores will allow Jill to receive her promotion?

Indicate all such sets.

(A) 3.0, 3.5, 4.75, 4.75

(B) 3.5, 4.75, 4.75, 5.0

(C) 3.25, 4.5, 4.75, 5.0

(D) 3.75, 4.5, 4.75, 5.0

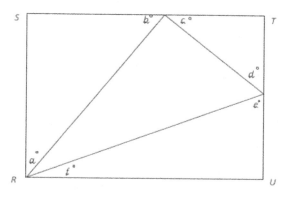

17. In the figure above, if *RSTU* is a rectangle, what is the value of $a + b + c + d + e + f$?

_____

_____ Degrees

18. If the probability of choosing 2 red marbles without replacement from a bag of only red and blue marbles is $3/55$ and there are 3 red marbles in the bag, what is the total number of marbles in the bag?

(A) 10

(B) 11

(C) 55

(D) 110

(E) 165

19. All first-year students at Red State University must take calculus, English composition, or both. If half of the 2,400 first-year students at Red State University take calculus and half do not, and one-third of those who take calculus also take English composition, how many students take English composition?

(A) 400

(B) 800

(C) 1,200

(D) 1,600

(E) 2,000

20. If $\dfrac{13!}{2^x}$ is an integer, which of the following represents all possible values of x ?

(A) $0 \leq x \leq 10$

(B) $0 < x < 9$

(C) $0 \leq x < 10$

(D) $1 \leq x \leq 10$

(E) $1 < x < 10$

Section 4 Verbal reasoning

30 Minutes

30 Questions

This section consists of five different types of questions: Sentence Completion, Analogy, Antonym, Text Completion with Two or Three Blanks and Reading Comprehension. To answer the questions, select the best answer from the answer choices given. Circle the letter or word(s) of your choice.

Directions for Sentence Completion Questions: The following sentences each contain one or two blanks, indicating that something has been left out of the sentence. Each answer choice contains one word or a set of words. Select the word or set of words that, when inserted in the blank(s), best fits the context of the sentence.

Example: Because of his   , Brian's guests felt very welcome and comfortable staying at his house for the weekend.

  (A) Animosity

  (B) Hospitality

  (C) Determination

  (D) Wittiness

  (E) Severity

Directions for Analogy Questions: The following questions contain a set of related words in capital letters and five answer choices. Each answer choice also contains a set of words. Select the set of words that represents a relationship similar to the original set of words.

Example: APPRENTICE: PLUMBER:

(A) player : coach

(B) child : parent

(C) student : teacher

(D) author : publisher

(E) intern : doctor

Directions for Antonym Questions: The following questions contain a word in capital letters and five answer choices. Each answer choice contains a word or phrase. Select the word or phrase that best expresses a meaning opposite to the word in capital letters.

Example: CREDULOUS:

(A) skeptical

(B) naive

(C) spontaneous

(D) sensitive

(E) discrete

Directions for Text Completion with Two or Three Blanks Questions: These questions consist of a short passage with two or three numbered blanks, indicating that something has been left out of the text. Select the word or set of words that, when inserted in the blanks, best completes the text.

Example: Experts believe that humans have ten trillion cells in their bodies that (i) _____any number of essential genetic elements; scientists often marvel at what incredible (ii)__would ensue should the cells become jumbled or misunderstand their purpose.

Blank (i)	Blank (ii)
Govern	Order
Organize	Method
Dislocate	Chaos

Directions for Reading Comprehension Questions: The passages in this section are followed by several questions. The questions correspond to information that is stated or implied in the passage. Read the passage and choose the best answer for each question.

Answer the questions in the order presented.

The Verbal section questions begin on the next page.

1. MEDICINE : DOSE ::

    (A) surgeon : scalpel

    (B) paper : ream

    (C) treatment : hospital

    (D) ocean : water

    (E) office : decor

2. ACCEPT : DEMUR ::

    (A) enact : revoke

    (B) deny : repel

    (C) mute : dispel

    (D) despise : annoy

    (E) reject : disdain

3. In addition to advising the school newspaper staff, Mr. Mathison also regularly...........the junior class regarding community service opportunities.

    (A) rallied against

    (B) counseled

    (C) argued with

    (D) suppressed

4.   I could barely follow the............story line; the numerous twists and turns in the plot made it extremely hard to comprehend.

    (A) convoluted

    (B) unambiguous

    (C) conventional

    (D) resolute

    (E) dependable

5.   GLACIER : ICE ::

    (A) beach : sand

    (B) mountain : clouds

    (C) ship : harbor

    (D) hammer : chisel

    (E) novel : characters

6.   CAPRICIOUS:

    (A) dogmatic

    (B) eccentric

    (C) steadfast

    (D) poignant

    (E) raucous

7.   GLIB:

    (A) pugnacious

    (B) gleeful

    (C) guileless

    (D) punctilious

    (E) flippant

8. COLLUSION : FRAUD ::

   (A) dissident : friend

   (B) eccentricity : normalcy

   (C) enigma : mistake

   (D) diatribe : insult

   (E) surplus : debit

9. INSULAR:

   (A) insolvent

   (B) cosmopolitan

   (C) ominous

   (D) biased

   (E) perceptible

10. PLETHORA:

   (A) rhetoric

   (B) presumption

   (C) mutiny

   (D) deficiency

   (E) figment

11. MALEVOLENT:

   (A) marred

   (B) meticulous

   (C) magnanimous

   (D) malcontent

   (E) malignant

12. DISCONCERTED:

   (A) composed

(B) miserly

(C) relentless

(D) sheepish

(E) perturbed

13.   REVIVE : EXHAUSTED ::

(A) reward : superior

(B) refer : adjacent

(C) replace : lost

(D) rejuvenate : drained

(E) resume : interrupted

14. Some teachers complained that the school board was, focusing on short-term goals while ignoring the long-term benefits of classroom reorganization.

(A) ambiguous

(B) myopic

(C) perceptive

(D) discerning

(E) replete

15.   The apparent rigidity of military discipline often (i) ....the surprising level of independent thinking expected of the modern officer. Combat situations often (ii) ....spur-of-the-moment decisions.

Blank (i)   Blank (ii)

Blank (i)	Blank (ii)
Belies	Defy
Impinges	Discourage
Supplants	Mandate
Negates	Banish
Mitigates	Emulate

16.   Certain members of my family continued to lead.........   lives,   often

indulging in wild and...............behavior.

    (A) chaotic . ... impulsive

    (B) temperate ....frenzied

    (C) moderate .... destructive

    (D) arbitrary ....leisurely

    (E) boisterous ....unpretentious

Line

(5)

(10)

Questions 17 and 18 are based on the following passage.

The Lincoln Memorial, located on the National Mall in Washington, D.C., is one of the most profound symbols of American democracy in the world. Dedicated in 1922, it won the prestigious Gold Medal of the American Institute of Architects for its architect, Henry Bacon. The physical presence of the memorial is awe- inspiring. There are a total of 36 Doric columns around the building, each representing one of the 36 states of the union at the time of Lincoln's death in 1865. Stones from various states were used in the construction of the memorial. The names of the 48 states in the Union at the time of the memorial's completion are carved on the outside walls. The north wall of the Lincoln Memorial boasts the sixteenth president's second inaugural address, while on the south wall, the Gettysburg Address is proudly carved. Above the statue of Abraham Lincoln are these words: "In this Temple, as in the hearts of the people for whom he saved the Union, the memory of Abraham Lincoln is enshrined forever."

17. The word *boasts* (line 9) most nearly means

    (A) to possess

    (B) to construct

    (C) to brag

    (D) to dedicate

    (E) to inaugurate

18. The passage suggests that the author would be most likely to agree with which of the following statements?

    (A) The Lincoln Memorial was constructed at a time when little was known about architecture.

    (B) The true meaning of the Lincoln Memorial is obscured by its architecture.

    (C) Most people who visit the Lincoln Memorial are unaware of its importance.

    (D) Since the completion of the Lincoln Memorial, few other memorials have been built that match its quality.

The size and significance of the Lincoln Memorial are equally impressive.

19. TACIT : EXPLICIT ::

    (A) lucid : muddled

    (B) negligible : obedient

    (C) odious : intact

    (D) pedantic : curious

    (E) wily : expert

20. Her disheveled clothing and   hair surprised me; Amanda's appearance is normally very polished and chic.

    (A) orderly

    (B) capacious

    (C) unkempt

    (D) formal

    (E) striking

Questions 21–24 are based on the following passage. Human reliance on information technology today is quickly becoming global. The technological developments in the areas of computing, networking, and software engineering have aided the transitions from paper to paperless transactions, and text and data media to multimedia. Today, speed, efficiency, and accuracy in the exchange of information have become primary tools for increasing productivity and innovation. Activities as diverse as health care, education, and manufacturing have come to depend on the generation, storage, and transmission of electronic information. Computers are not only used extensively to perform the industrial and economic functions of society but are also used to provide many services upon which human life depends. Medical treatment, air traffic control, and national security are a few examples. Even a small glitch in the operation of these systems can put human lives in danger. Computers are also used to store confidential data of a political, social, economic, or personal nature. This fairly recent and progressive dependence on computer technology signals a real danger for the human race.

Current computer systems offer new opportunities for lawbreaking and the potential to commit traditional types of crimes in nontraditional ways. For example, the threat of identity theft is magnified by our reliance on computers to assist us in everyday activities such as shopping and paying bills. Identity theft refers to all types of crime in which someone wrongfully obtains and uses another person's personal data by way of fraud or deception, typically for economic gain. By making personal and credit information available on the Internet, people open themselves up to the possibility of a criminal obtaining this information and using it for nefarious purposes. This is but one instance of the negative impact that overreliance on computer technology can have on society.

As humans continue to make technological advances, so too do they rely more heavily upon those innovations. This is a dangerous progression that must be tempered with common sense and self-restraint. We cannot allow computer technology to control too many aspects of our lives, lest we become victims of our own ingenuity.

21. The primary purpose of the passage is to

    (A) challenge a commonly held belief regarding identity fraud

    (B) discuss some potentially devastating effects of our dependence on computers

    (C) suggest ways in which the human race can reduce its dependence on technology

    (D) evaluate the pros and cons of computer technology

    (E) defend a controversial perspective on the transmission of electronic data

22. The author most likely uses the phrase "a small glitch" (line 11) in order to

    (A) acknowledge the fact that human reliance on computer technology is completely safe

    (B) emphasize the idea that it is dangerous for humans to rely so heavily on computer technology

(C) cast doubt on the accuracy of any personal data collected on the Internet by criminals

(D) criticize human technological advances in the areas of education, medicine, and national security

(E) disprove the theory that computer technology is unnecessary for human advancement

23. The passage suggests that the author would be most likely to agree with which of the following statements?

(A) Human dependence on computer technology has never been known to advance the species.

(B) Human dependence on computer technology should never be allowed under any circumstances.

(C) Human dependence on computer technology is a key component in the advancement of the species.

(D) Human dependence on computer technology cannot be accurately measured.

(E) Human dependence on computer technology can sometimes have a negative impact on society.

24. Each of the following is mentioned in the passage as a potential danger resulting from greater reliance on computer technology EXCEPT:

I.   The transmission of electronic data

II.   Increased opportunity for criminal activity

III. A drastic reduction in national security

(A) I only

(B) I and II only

(C) I and III only

(D) II and III only

(E) I, II, and III

Questions 25 and 26 are based on the following passage.

This passage is adapted from *The American Republic: Constitution, Tendencies, and Destiny* by O. A. Brownson, © 1866.

The ancients summed up the whole of human wisdom in the maxim "Know Thyself," and certainly there is for an individual no more important and no more difficult knowledge, than knowledge of himself. Nations are only individuals on a larger scale. They have a life, an individuality, a reason, a conscience, and instincts of their own, and have the same general laws of development and growth, and, perhaps, of decay, as the individual man. Equally important, and no less difficult than for the individual, is it for a nation to know itself, understand its own existence, its own powers and faculties, rights and duties, constitution, instincts, tendencies, and destiny. A nation has a spiritual as well as a material existence, a moral as well as a physical existence, and is subjected to internal as well as external conditions of health and virtue, greatness and grandeur, which it must in some measure understand and observe, or become lethargic and infirm, stunted in its growth, and end in premature decay and death.

Among nations, no one has more need of full knowledge of itself than the United States, and no one has, to this point, had less. It has hardly had a distinct consciousness of its own national existence, and has lived the naive life of the child, with no severe trial, till the recent civil war, to throw it back on itself and compel it to reflect on its own constitution, its own separate existence, individuality, tendencies, and end. The defection of the slaveholding States, and the fearful struggle that has followed for national unity and integrity, have brought the United States at once to a distinct recognition of itself, and forced it to pass from thoughtless, careless, heedless, reckless adolescence to grave and reflecting manhood. The nation has been suddenly compelled to study itself, and from now on must act from reflection, understanding, science, and statesmanship, not from instinct, impulse, passion, or caprice, knowing well what it does, and why it does it. The change that four years of civil war have wrought in the nation is great, and is sure to give it the seriousness, the gravity, and the dignity it has so far lacked.

25. Which of the following statements best summarizes the main point of the first paragraph?

(A) Understanding one's own strengths and weaknesses is a difficult yet important task, not only for individuals, but for nations as a whole.

(B) The spirituality of individuals should be dictated by the nation's government.

(C) The comparing of a nation to a person is inaccurate and leads only to confusion and misrepresentation.

(D) The United States was founded upon a principle of law that originated from the ancient world.

(E) A nation's moral existence is governed by external conditions only.

26. The author's argument is developed primarily by the use of

(A) an example of one nation's success

(B) an analogy between man and nation

(C) a critique of the United States Constitution

(D) a warning against civil war

(E) a personal account of self-realization

27.　　The editors of the magazine are often criticized for the............... of their opinion column, which frequently............ from one side of an issue to the other.

(A) monotony .....continues

(B) ingenuity ....settles

(C) unpredictability.........scuttles

(D) inconsistency ....vacillates

(E) rigidity ....dithers

28. DEPLORABLE:

(A) eligible

(B) miserable

(C) irreproachable

(D) reprehensible

(E) intractable

29. CIRCUMSPECT:

(A) intricate

(B) reckless

(C) dissonant

(D) formative

(E) prudent

30. RESERVOIR : LAKE ::

(A) dam : river

(B) hub : wheel

(C) canal : waterway

(D) bank : stream

(E) window : door

Section 5: Quantitative reasoning

General Information

Numbers: All the numbers shown in this section are real numbers.

Figures: Assume that the position of all points, angles, etc. are in the order shown and the measures of angles are positive,

All figures lie in a plane unless otherwise stated.

All straight lines can be assumed to be straight.

Note that geometric figures are *not necessarily drawn to scale*. Do not try to estimate lengths and sizes of figures in order to answer questions.

Directions

Multiple-Choice Questions—Select One Answer

Select one answer choice from a list of five choices.

Multiple-Choice Questions—Select One or More Answers

Select one or more answer choices following the directions given.

You must select all of the correct answer choices and no others in order to earn credit for the question.

If the question specifies how many answer choices to select, you must select that number of choices.

Numeric Entry Questions

Indicate your answer in the box provided with the question.

Equivalent forms of an answer, such as 1.5 and 1.50, are all correct.

You do not have to reduce fractions to lowest terms.

Quantitative Comparisons

These questions present two quantities, Quantity A and Quantity B. Information about one or both of the quantities may be provided in the space above the two quantities. You must compare the two quantities and choose

- if Quantity A is greater
- if Quantity B is greater
- if the two quantities are equal
- if the relationship between the two quantities cannot be determined

These questions present two quantities, Quantity A and Quantity B. Information about one or both of the quantities may be provided in the space above the two quantities. You must compare the two quantities and choose

- if Quantity A is greater
- if Quantity B is greater
- if the two quantities are equal
- if the relationship between the two quantities cannot be determined1. $a^2 - b^2 > 1$

Quantity A	Quantity B
a.	b.

(A) Quantity A is greater.

(B) Quantity B is greater.

(C) The two quantities are equal.

(D) The relationship cannot be determined from the information given.

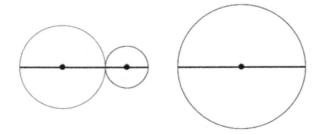

2.

In the diagram, the sum of the diameters of the two smaller circles is equivalent to the diameter of the larger circle.

Quantity A	Quantity B
The circumference of the larger circle	The sum of the circumferences of the smaller circles

(A) Quantity A is greater.

(B) Quantity B is greater.

(C) The two quantities are equal.

(D) The relationship cannot be determined from the information given.

3. $x^3 > x^4$

Quantity A	Quantity B
X	0

4. $b2c < 0$

$abc > 0$

Quantity A	Quantity B
AB	0

(A) Quantity A is greater.

(B) Quantity B is greater.

(C) The two quantities are equal.

(D) The relationship cannot be determined from the information given.

5. The probability that a certain event will occur is x. The probability that the event will not occur is y.

Quantity A	Quantity B
X+y	1

(A) Quantity A is greater.

(B) Quantity B is greater.

(C) The two quantities are equal.

(D) The relationship cannot be determined from the information given.

6. n and q are positive integers, and n is a multiple of 5

Quantity A	Quantity B
q^{n-5}	$q^{n/5}$

(A) Quantity A is greater.

(B) Quantity B is greater.

(C) The two quantities are equal.

(D) The relationship cannot be determined from the information given.

7. ABC and DEF are triangles with sides of given lengths.

Quantity A	Quantity B
The size of angle ABC	The size of angle DEF

(A) Quantity A is greater.

(B) Quantity B is greater.

(C) The two quantities are equal.

(D) The relationship cannot be determined from the information given.

8. The retail price of a bookshelf is y dollars. The retailer will either add $5 to the retail price and then mark the price down by z%, or will mark the price down by z%, and then add $5 to the new price.

Quantity A	Quantity B

Quantity A

The price of the bookshelf after the retailer adds $5 to the retail price and then marks the new price down by z%.

Quantity B

The price of the bookshelf after the retailer marks the original price down by z%, and then adds $5 to the new price.

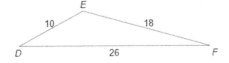

(A) Quantity A is greater.

(B) Quantity B is greater.

(C) The two quantities are equal.

(D) The relationship cannot be determined from the information given.

8. The retail price of a bookshelf is y dollars. The retailer will either add $5 to the retail price and then mark the price down by z%, or will mark the price down by z%, and then add $5 to the new price.

Quantity A

The price of the bookshelf after the retailer adds $5 to the retail price and then marks the new price down by z%. Quantity B.

Quantity B

The price of the bookshelf after the retailer marks the original price down by z%, and then adds $5 to the new price.

(A) Quantity A is greater.

(B) Quantity B is greater.

(C) The two quantities are equal.

(D) The relationship cannot be determined from the information given.

9. $4a^2 - 4b^2$ is equivalent to which of the following?

(A) $(2a - 2b)(2a - 2b)$

(B) $(4a - 4b)(4a - 4b)$

(C) $(2a + 2b)(2a - 2b)$

(D) *(2a + 2b)(a − b)*

(E) *(4a + 2b)(4a − 2b)*

10. If each of the sides of a certain square is doubled in length, by what factor will the area of the square increase?

11. On Tuesday, a salesman made four sales. On the first three sales, the salesman received a commission of $2,100, $1,500, and $1,800. If the salesman's average commission for all four sales was $2,000, what was the salesman's commission on the fourth sale?

(A) $2,100

(B) $2,300

(C) $2,400

(D) $2,500

(E) $2,600

12. If $2a < 6$, and $3b > 27$, then $b − a$ can equal all of the following but not which value?

(A) 6

(B) 7

(C) 8

(D) 9

(E) 10

13.

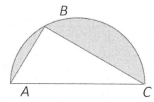

Triangle ABC is inscribed in the semicircle above. If the length of side *AB* is 10, and the length of side *BC* is 24, what is the area of the shaded region?

(A) 169π

(B) 84.5π

(C) $169\pi - 120$

(D) $84.5\pi - 120$

(E) 120

14. An asteroid travels through space at a constant rate of 2.6 million feet per day. If the distance between the asteroid and a certain planet is 10.2 million feet, approximately how many seconds will it take the asteroid to reach the planet?

(A) 80,000

(B) 120,000

(C) 200,000

(D) 250,000

(E) 350,000

15.

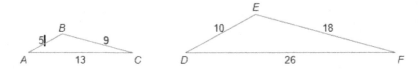

Percentage Change in Student

Majors at University X

Major	2015	2017
Biology	−12	8
Psychology	−10	10
Mathematics	6	11
English	−3	−10
Philosophy	11	−3

16. If 1,000 students majored in Philosophy in 2015, how many students majored in Philosophy in 2017?

(A) 1,060

(B) 1,077

(C) 1,073

(D) 1,078

(E) 1,133

17. Based on the chart provided, which of the following statements must be true? (Indicate all that apply.)

    (A) The number of students who majored in Psychology in 2017 was less than the number of students who majored in Psychology in 2015.

    (B) The number of students who majored in Mathematics in 2017 was more than 17% greater than the number of students who majored in Mathematics in 2015.

    (C) In 2017, more students majored in Mathematics than in any of the other majors in the chart.17. If the number of students who majored in Biology in 2015 was double the number of students who majored in English in 2015, then the number of students who majored in Biology in 2017 was what percent greater than the number of students who majored in English in 2017? Round your answer to the nearest integer.

18. The population of State X is double that of State Y. If the population concentration (people per square mile) of State X is triple that of State Y, then what is the ratio of the area of State X to the area of State Y?

19. If x and y are unique nonzero integers such that $x + y = 0$, then one of the below is untrue, which one is it?

    (A) $|x| = |y|$

    (B) $x < y$

    (C) $xy > 0$

    (D) $x^2 + y^2 = 0$

    (E) $x^3 + y^3 = 0$

20. A survey of voter preferences showed that, rounded to the nearest tenths digit, 14.2% of voters expressed a preference for an independent candidate. If 80,000 voters responded to this survey, which of the following could equal the number of voters who expressed a preference for an independent candidate? (Indicate all that apply.)

(A) 11,315

(B) 11,321

(C) 11,390

(D) 11,399

(E) 11,400

Section 6: Verbal reasoning

For questions 1 through 6, select one entry for each blank from the corresponding column of choices. Fill all blanks in the way that best completes the text.

1.   Despite what ....philosophies of child- rearing suggest, there is no imperative that the day-to-day action of raising a child be simple, unambiguous, and unchanging—no requirement, in other words, ensures that life follows philosophy.

   (A) Inexact

   (B) Aggressive

   (C) Random

   (D) Shameless

   (E) Systematic

2. All the greatest chess players in the world know that it is folly to be (i)................when facing a formidable opponent, as stubbornness will almost surely lead to mistakes that force a player to (ii) ....to the prevailing strategy of their opponent.

   (A) Blank (i)   Blank (ii)

   (B) finicky   capitulate

   (C) obdurate   dissent

   (D) vituperative   repudiate

3 The novel emphasizes the innate (i) .... of all humans, showing how each and every character within the narrative is, ultimately, (ii) .... This motif becomes tiresome due to its (iii) ...., however, as character after character is bribed, either explicitly or implicitly, into giving up his or her supposedly cherished beliefs.

4 Although pirating software, such as borrowing a friend's copy of an installation CD or downloading software from unapproved sources is (i)............. , many people continue to do so (ii)................., almost as if they were unaware that such acts amount to theft.

(A) Blank (i)   Blank (ii)

(B) uncommon   savagely

(C) illegal   sensibly

(D) difficult   unabashedly

5. Having squandered his life's savings on unprofitable business ventures, the ....entrepreneur was forced to live in squalor.

(A) former

(B) unlikely

(C) insolvent

(D) perturbed

(E) eccentric

6. Teachers of composition urge their students to

(i)............... in their writing and instead use clear, simple language. Why use (ii)..............vocabulary when a (iii)................phrasing conveys one's meaning so much more effectively?

Blank (i)	Blank (ii)	Blank (iii)
exscind obloquy	recreant	arcane
eschew obfuscation	redolent	limpid
evince ossification	recondite	droll

Blank (i)	Blank (ii)	Blank (iii)
zealousness	adroit	redundancy
corruptibility	cunning	triviality
optimism	venal	subtlety

For each of Questions 7 to 11, select one answer choice unless otherwise instructed.

Questions 7 through 8 are based on the following reading passage.

Neurobiologists have never questioned that axon malfunction plays a role in neurological disorders, but the nature of the relationship has been a matter of speculation. George Bartzokis's neurological research at UCLA suggests that many previously poorly understood disorders such as Alzheimer's disease may be explained by examining the role of the chemical compound myelin.

Myelin is produced by oligodendrocyte cells as a protective sheathing for axons within the nervous system. As humans mature and their neurochemistry's grow more complex, oligodendrocyte cells produce increasing amounts of myelin to protect the byzantine circuitry inside our nervous systems. An apt comparison may be to the plastic insulation around copper wires. Bereft of myelin, certain areas of the brain may be left vulnerable to short circuiting, resulting in such disorders as ADHD, schizophrenia, and autism.

7. Consider each of the choices separately and select all that apply.

It can be inferred from the passage that the author would be most likely to agree with which of the following statements regarding the role of myelin?

(A) The levels of myelin in the brain can contribute to the neurological health of individuals.

(B) Increasing the levels of myelin in the brain can reverse the effects of neurological damage.

(C) The levels of myelin in the brain are not fixed throughout the lifetime of an individual.

8. In the context in which it appears, byzantine most nearly means

(A) devious

(B) intricate

(C) mature

(D) beautiful

(E) electronic

9   .The cost of operating many small college administrative offices is significantly reduced when the college replaces its heavily compensated administrative assistants with part-time work-study students whose earnings are partially subsidized by the government.

Therefore, large universities should follow suit, as they will see greater financial benefits than do small colleges.

In the above argument it is assumed that

(A) replacing administrative assistants with work- study students is more cost-effective for small colleges than for large universities

(B) large universities usually depend upon small colleges for development of money-saving strategies

(C) the financial gains realized by large universities would not be as great were they to use non-work-study students in place of the administrative assistants

(D) work-study students at large universities could feasibly fulfill a similar or greater proportion of administrative assistant jobs than what they could at small colleges

(E) the smaller the college or university, the easier it is for that college or university to control costs

Questions 10 through 11 are based on the following reading passage.

The nineteenth century marked a revolutionary change in the way wealth was perceived in England. As landed wealth gave way to monied wealth, investments became increasingly speculative.

A popular investment vehicle was the three- The nineteenth century marked a revolutionary change in the way wealth was perceived in England. As landed wealth gave way to monied wealth, investments became increasingly speculative.

A popular investment vehicle was the three-percent consol which took its name from the fact that it paid three pounds on a hundred pound investment. The drawback to the consol was that once issued, there was no easy way for the government to buy back the debt. To address the problem, the British government instituted a sinking fund, using tax revenue to buy back the bonds in the open market. The fact that the consol had no fixed maturity date ensured that any change in interest rate was fully reflected in the capital value of the bond. The often wild fluctuation of interest rates ensured the consol's popularity with speculative traders.

10 .Which of the following best describes the relationship of the first paragraph of the passage to the passage as a whole?

A. It provides a generalization which is later supported in the passage.

B. It provides an antithesis to the author's main argument.

C. It briefly compares two different investment strategies.

D. It explains an investment vehicle that is later examined in greater detail.

E. It provides a historical framework by which the nature of the nineteenth-century investor can more easily be understood.

11 .In the second paragraph, select the sentence that describes a solution to a problem.

(A) Viscous

(B) Vossified

(C) rarefied

(D) estimable

(E) copious

(F) meager

For questions 12 through 15, select the two answer choices that, when used to complete the sentence, fit the meaning of the sentence as a whole and produce completed sentences that are alike in meaning.

12. Owing to a combination of its proximity and .... Atmosphere, mars is the only planet in our solar system whose surface details can be discerned from earth.

13. Using the hardships of the Joad family as a model, John Steinbeck's The Grapes of Wrath effectively demonstrated how one clan's struggles epitomized the ....experienced by an entire country.

(A) reticence

(B) adversity

(C) repudiation

(D) quiescence

(E) verisimilitude

(F) tribulation

14. The Mayan pyramid of Kukulkan is more than just.......... edifice; this imposing structure was built to create a chirping echo whenever people clap their hands on the staircase. This echo sounds just like the chirp of the Quetzal, a bird which is sacred in the Mayan culture.

- (A) a venerable
- (B) a humble
- (C) a beguiling
- (D) an august
- (E) a specious
- (F) a prosaic

15 . Some wealthy city-dwellers become enchanted with the prospect of trading their hectic schedules for a bucolic life in the countryside, and they buy property with a pleasant view of farmland—only to find the stench of the livestock so ....that they move back to the city.

- (A) bovine
- (B) pastoral
- (C) noisome
- (D) atavistic
- (E) olfactory
- (F) mephitic

For each of Questions 16 to 20, select one answer choice unless otherwise instructed.

Questions 16 through 18 are based on the following reading passage.

Often the most influential developments initially appear to be of minor significance. Consider the development of the basic stirrup for example.

Without stirrups horse and rider are, in terms of force, separate entities; lances can be used from horseback, but only by throwing or stabbing, and mounted warriors gain only height and mobility. In medieval times, A lance couched under the rider's arm, unifying the force of rider and weapon, would throw its wielder backwards off the horse at impact. Stirrups unify lance, rider, and horse into a force capable of unprecedented violence. This development left unusually clear archaeological markers: With lethality assured, lances evolved barbs meant to slow progress after impact, lest the weight of body pull rider from horse. The change presaged the dominance of mounted combat, and increasingly expensive equipment destroyed the venerable ideal of freeman warriors. New technology demanded military aristocracy, and chivalric culture bore its marks for a millennium.

16   . The primary purpose of the passage is to

  (A) discuss the influence of a recent archeological discovery

  (B) explore the societal significance of a technological innovation

  (C) assess the state of research in a given field

  (D) lament the destruction of certain social ideals

  (E) explicate the physics of combat artillery

17. It can be inferred from the passage that the author believes which of the following about innovations in military technology?

Their study merits additional research.

They had more lasting influence than did those of the ancient world.

Most of them had equally far-reaching repercussions.

Prior to their application, the military value of horses was considered insignificant.

Many of them are archaeologically ambiguous.

18. Select the sentence in the passage in which the author cites the physical effects of a technological innovation being discussed as an example of a previous generalization.

Questions 19 through 20 are based on the following reading passage.

Few mathematical constructs seem as conceptually simple as that of randomness. According to the traditional definition, a number is random if it is chosen purely as the result of a probabilistic mechanism such as the roll of a fair die. In their ground breaking work regarding complexity and the limitations of formal systems, mathematicians Gregory Chaitin and A.N. Kolmogorov force us to consider this last claim more closely.

Consider two possible outcomes of throwing a fair die three times: first, 1, 6, and 2; second 3, 3, and 3. Now let us construct two three-member sets based on the results. Though the first set {1,6,2}—intuitively seems more random than the second—{3,3,3}, they are each as likely to occur, and thus according to the accepted definition, must be considered equally random. This unwelcome result prompts Chaitin and Kolmogorov to suggest the need for a new standard of randomness, one that relies on the internal coherence of the set as opposed to its origin.

19. Which of the following best describes the organization of the passage as whole?

A concept is introduced; a traditional definition is put forward; a thought experiment is described; a new definition is proposed; the traditional definition is amended as a result.

A concept is introduced; a traditional definition is supported by authorities; a thought experiment is described; the implications of the experiment are discussed.

A concept is introduced; a traditional definition is considered and rejected; a thought experiment is described; a new definition is proposed.

A concept is introduced; a traditional definition is called into question; a thought experiment is described; the implications of the experiment are discussed.

A concept is introduced; authorities are called in to reevaluate a definition; a thought experiment is described; the implications of the experiment are considered and rejected.

20. Consider each of the choices separately and select all that apply.

Which of the following is an inference made in the passage above?

The results of the same probabilistic mechanism will each be as likely as the other to occur.

According to the traditional definition of randomness, two numbers should be considered equally random if they result from the same probabilistic mechanism.

Different probabilistic mechanisms are likely to result in similar outcomes.

Answers

Section 1

Compare your response to the advice in the analytical writing area to calculate your score.

Section 2

Compare your response to the advice in the analytical writing area to calculate your score.

Section 3

1. A

Point C has the same x–coordinate as point D, so s = 8. Point C also has the same y-coordinate as point B, so t = 7. That means that Quantity A is greater.

2. A

The punch is made with two parts soda and three parts ice cream. This means that in one mixture if you added two parts of soda, then that's 4 × 2 = 8 parts sugar and 5 × 2 = 10 parts citric acid. If you added three parts ice cream, then that's 3 × 3 = 9 parts sugar and 2 × 3 = 6 parts salt. There's 8 + 9 = 17 total parts sugar and 10 + 6 = 16 total parts citric acid. There's more sugar than citric acid.

3. B

If you Plug In 5 for x, the total for the 5 days already in the set is 350; after adding the additional 75 degree temperature, the new total is 425, and the new average is , which reduces to 70 , which is less than 71 degrees. This means that x cannot equal 5 and thus we can eliminate choice (C). If x = 4, then the total for the 4 days would be 280; after adding

75, the new total would be 355, and the new average would be , which reduces to 71. Thus we can eliminate choice (A). The answer is choice (B).

4. D

Because ΔQRS is isosceles, side RS must be equal to one of the other sides, and x could measure 4 or 7. Thus, the perimeter could be 4 + 4 + 7 = 15, or the perimeter could be 4 + 7 + 7 = 18. You can't tell if the perimeter is greater or less than 17, and, thus, the answer is choice (D). Remember: If it doesn't say "Drawn to scale," you can't assume it is!

5. B

Remember that a normal distribution curve has divisions of 34 percent, 14 percent, and 2 percent on each side of the mean. 80 out of 500 is 16 percent, or 14 percent + 2 percent, and 10 out of 500 is 2 percent. Draw a normal distribution curve and label it. There are three standard deviations between 92 and 56, so 92 − 56 = 36, and 36 ÷ 3 = 12. The mean is 92 − 12 = 80, which is smaller than Quantity B.

6. C

Plug In numbers for the sides. Let AD = 4, so EG = 8. Let I = 3. The area of ABCD = 3 × 4 = 12, and the area of EFG = (3 × 8) = 12. The two quantities can be equal, so eliminate answer choices (A) and (B). Try changing your numbers, and you will see that the two quantities will always be equal.

7. B

FOIL out the equation given, and you'll get $(3x - 4y)(3x + 4y) = 9x^2 - 16y^2$, so Quantity A is 2. Quantity B is therefore bigger, and the answer is (B).

8. C

Solve for a by adding 2 to each side to get 8a = 24. Divide by 8 to ɪnd a = 3. Plug a = 3 into the second equation to ɪnd 4(3) − 1 = 12 − 1 = 11. Alternatively, you could save yourself some time by noticing that 8a − 2 is 2(4a − 1). If 2(4a −1) = 22, divide by 2 to get 4a − 1 = 11. 9. 56 Twenty percent of the sweaters in the store are white, so there are 200 × = 40 white sweaters. There are 200 − 40 = 160 sweaters remaining. Of the remaining sweaters, 160 × = 64 are brown. That means that 160 − 64 = 96 are blue. There are 96 − 40 = 56 more blue sweaters than white sweaters.

10. D

Because 4^{12} is a common factor of both 4^{13} and 4^{12}, you can rewrite the numerator as 4^{12} (4 − 1). Now look at the whole fraction: . You can divide 4^{12} by 4^{11}, leaving you with 41(4 − 1). Now the calculation should be much easier. 4 × 3 = 12, choice (D).

11. D

Refer to the right side and the left side of the "Subscription to Newsmagazine x, 1970-1985" chart. In 1980, Newsmagazine x accounted for 14.6 percent of newsmagazine subscriptions, and it had 7,000 subscriptions.

12. B

In 1981, Newsmagazine z accounted for 9,400 out of 57,000 newsmagazine subscriptions. Therefore, Newsmagazine z accounted for approximately 9,000 out of 57,000, or , of the nationwide newsmagazine subscriptions.

13. D

In 1970, there were 1,500 subscriptions to Newsmagazine x, which accounted for approximately 25 percent of total nationwide subscriptions. Total nationwide subscriptions in 1970, then, were equal to about 6,000 (25 percent of total nationwide subscriptions = 1,500). Using the same process, total nationwide subscriptions in 1971 were equal to about 9,000 (30 percent of total nationwide subscriptions = 2,600). The percent increase between 1970 and 1971 is or , or 50 percent.

14. C

In 1973, Newsmagazine x had 3,300 subscriptions, or 20.5 percent of the total number of newsmagazine subscriptions. Set up the calculation to ɹnd the total: 3,300 = . Solve it to find that x = 16,000.

15. C

a = 27 × = 3, and x = 6 × = 2. Find (12)(3−x)(15)(2−a) = (12)(3−2)(15) (2−3) = . Now, reduce: .

16. B and D

Use the Average Pie to ɹnd that Jill's mean of 3.75 for 8 evaluations gives her a current total of 3.75 × 8 = 30 points. Use the Average Pie to ɹnd that if she needs an average of 4.0 for 12 scores, she needs 4.0 × 12 = 48 total points. Jill still needs 48 − 30 = 18 points. Her four remaining scores must total 18 or greater. Only answers (B) and (D) have a total of at least 18.

17. 270

Your best bet is to plug in values for all the angles, keeping in mind that those inside the triangle must add up to 180°, the ones along BC must add up to 180, the ones along CD must add up to 180°, and the ones at A must add up to 90°. Then add up the marked angles.

18. B

Plug In The Answers starting with choice (C). If the total is 55, then the probability would be , which does not equal . The denominator is too large, so try choice (B). If the total is 11, then the probability is , which reduces to .

19. D

Use the Group formula: Total = Group1 + Group2 − Both + Neither. In this problem the total is 2,400. The question also states that 1,200 students (half of the total) take calculus, so that is Group1; one-third of that group (400) take both calculus and English. Because every student takes calculus or English or both, the Neither group is zero. Solve for the number of students who take English by plugging these numbers into the group formula: 2400 = 1200 + Group2 − 400. The number of students who take English is 1,600, or choice (D).

20. D

To solve this expression you need to break apart the factorial of 13 to the common prime number in the denominator, in this case the number 2. 13! can be expressed as 13 × 12 × 11 × 10 × 9 × 8 × 7 × 6 × 5 × 4 × 3 × 2 × 1. When you break apart this factorial into its prime numbers you are left with $13 \times 11 \times 7 \times 5^2 \times 3^5 \times 2^{10}$. For a fraction to result in an integer, the denominator of the fraction must share at least one prime factor with the numerator, so at minimum there needs to be one 2, so $1 \le x$. Eliminate (A), (B), and (C). The number of two's that the denominator can have cannot exceed 10 because that is the greatest number of two's in the numerator, so $x \le 10$. The correct answer is (D).

Section 4

1. B	16. A
2. A	17. A
3. B	18. E
4. A	19. A
5. A	20. C
6. C	21. B
7. C	22. B
8. D	23. E
9. B	24. A
10. D	25. A
11. C	26. B
12. A	27. D
13. D	28. C
14. B	29. B
15. Belies, Mandate	30. C

Section 5

1.   D Consider values that satisfy the given information. Case 1: $a = 2$, $b = 1$. In this case, $a > b$. Case 2: $a = -2$, $b = 1$. In this case, $a < b$. A relationship cannot be determined.

2.   C Choose values. Let the diameter of the larger circle = 10. In this case, the circumference of the larger circle is 10π. Let the diameter of the medium-sized circle be 6 and the diameter of the smaller circle be 4. In this case, the circumference of the smaller circle is 6π, and the circumference of the smaller circle is 4π. $6\pi + 4\pi = 10\pi$. The two quantities are equal.

3. D Test different numbers that would satisfy the prompt.   2

4   B Deduce what you can from the given information. The first inequality:

$b2$ must be positive because of the even exponent. Thus, if $b2c < 0$, then $c < 0$. Now, for the second inequality: If $c < 0$, and $abc > 0$, then $ab < 0$. Thus, Quantity B is greater.

5. C Since x and y are mutually exclusive, the sum of their probabilities must be 1.

6. D **Choose** numbers. If $q = 1$ and $n = 5$, then the value of both quantities is 1. If $q = 2$ and $n = 10$, then the value of quantity A is greater. A relationship cannot be determined.

7. C Note that each side of the larger triangle is double the corresponding side of the smaller triangle. These are thus similar triangles. One property of similar triangles is that corresponding angles are equal. Since angles ABC and DEF are opposite the largest side of their respective triangles, the measurement of these angles must be equal.

8. B Choose values. Let $y = 100$, and let $z = 20$. Now, evaluate Quantity A. With these values, a \$5 increase will lead to a bookshelf that costs \$105. After a 20% discount, the price of the bookshelf will be $.8(105) = 84$. Now, evaluate Quantity B. With these values, a 20% reduction in the retail price will result in a new price of $.8(100) = 80$. $80 + 5 = 85$. Quantity B is greater.

9. C The expression in the question is in the form of $x^2 - y^2$, where $4a^2$ corresponds to x^2 and $4b2$ corresponds to $y2$. Since $x2 - y2$ factors to $(x + y)(x - y)$, $4a^2 - 4b^2$ factors to $(2a)^2 - (2b)^2 = (2a + 2b)(2a - 2b)$.

10. 4 plug in numbers. Let the original side length of the square = 3. In this case, the original area is 9. If the length of each side is doubled, then the length of each side is 6 and the corresponding area is $62 = 36$. $\frac{36}{9} = 4$

11. E $2,600 was the salesman's commission on the fourth sale. Since the average of the four commissions is $2,000, the total must be $2,000 × 4 = $8,000. Subtracting the total of the other three commissions from $8,000 gives the commission on the fourth sale.

12. A First, isolate each variable. $2a < 6 \rightarrow a < 3$. $3b > 27 \rightarrow b > 9$. Now, assume that $a = 3$ and $b = 9$. In this case, $b - a = 9 - 3 = 6$. Since $a < 3$ and $b > 9$, the difference between the two must *be greater* than 6. Thus, 6 is not a possible value for $b - a$.

13. D Since triangle ABC is inscribed in a semicircle, it must be a right triangle. The area of the triangle is thus $\frac{1}{2} \times 10 \times 24 = 120$. Using the Pythagorean Theorem, the diameter of the circle = $AC = 26$. The area of the circle is thus $(\pi) r2 = (\pi)132 = (\pi)169$. The area of the semicircle is thus $\frac{169\pi}{2} = 84.5\pi$. The area of the shaded region = area of the semicircle − area of the triangle. This can be expressed as $84.5\pi - 120$.

14. E Plug the given values into the R × T = D formula. The rate is 2.6 million feet per day and the distance is 10.2 million feet. Thus: 2.6 million × T = 10.2 million → T = $\frac{10.2 \text{ million}}{}$ = approximately 4 days. Now, convert days to 2.6 million seconds. 1 day = 24 hours = 60(24) minutes = 60(60)(24) seconds = 86,400 seconds. So, the number of seconds in 4 days is 86,400 × 4 = 345,600 seconds. The closest answer is 350,000.

15. B The number of students majoring in Philosophy in 2015 was 1.11(1,000) = 1,110. The number of students majoring in Philosophy in 2017 was thus (.97)(1,110) = 1,076.7 or approximately 1,077.

16.A and B The easiest way to confirm each choice is to plug in numbers.

Choice A: Choose 1,000 for the number of Psychology majors in 2015. The number of Psychology majors in 2017 was thus 1,000(.9)(1.1) = 990. Choice A is correct.

Choice B: Choose 1,000 for the number of Mathematics majors in 2015. The number of Mathematics majors in 2017 was thus 1,000(1.06)(1.11) = 1,176. The change was 176. 176 is more than 17% of 1,000, Thus, choice B is correct.

Choice C: We have no values for any of the majors, so we cannot infer any relationships about the number of students in each major.

17.117% Choose values. Let the number of English majors in 2015 = 1,000. The number of biology majors in 2015 was thus 2,000. The number of Biology majors in 2017 was thus (2,000)(.88)(1.08) = 1,900.8. The number of English majors in 2017 was (1,000)(.97)(.9) = 873. Now, use the percent greater formula: % greater = % of − 100%. Plug in the numbers: (1,900.8/873) × 100 − 100% = 117%.

18. $\frac{2}{3}$ Plug in numbers: Let 1,200 = population of State X and 600 = population of State Y. Let the population concentration of State X = 12, and the population concentration of State Y = 4. The area of State X is thus $\frac{\text{population}}{\text{area}} = \frac{1,200}{\text{area}} = 12 \rightarrow$ area = 100. The area of State Y is thus $\frac{\text{population}}{\text{area}} = \frac{600}{\text{area}} = 4 \rightarrow$ area = 150.

Area area

The ratio of the area of State X to the area of State Y is thus $\frac{100}{150} = \frac{2}{3}$.

19. C and D If $x + y = 0$, and neither x nor $y = 0$, then it must be the case that x and y are different numbers with the same absolute value. For example, $x = -2$ and $y = 2$. Based on this example, choices A and B are possible. For choice C to be possible, x and y would have to have the same sign. But they cannot have the same sign since they must cancel each other out. Choice C cannot be true and is thus a possible answer. Choice D cannot be true because any non-zero number raised to an even exponent will yield a positive result. Positive + positive > 0. Choice E is always true, since odd exponents preserve the sign of the base. Because x and y have different signs, x3 and y3 will also have different signs.

20. B, C, and D If the percentage, when rounded to the nearest tenth, is 14.2%, then the actual percentage, p, is such that $14.15 \le p \le 14.249$. We can use this percentage range to yield a range for the number of voters who expressed a preference for an independent candidate. The lower bound will be 14.15% of 80,000 = 11,320. The upper bound will be 14.249% of 80,000 = 11,399.2. Any value that falls between these two endpoints will be an answer. Among the choices, the values that fall in this range are B, C, and D.

Section 6

1. Systematic

The clue is "simple, unambiguous, and unchanging." The trigger word is "in other words." The trigger word maintains the direction of the clue. Therefore, a word that means regimented. Systematic is the best match.

2. Obdurate and capitulate.

Try working with the second blank first. The second blank is talking about what a player will be forced to do if they are stubborn. The clue is that the mistakes the player makes will lead to the prevailing strategy of their opponent. Because of these clues, we know that a word that means "to give in" would be a good match. Capitulate is the only word that works as dissent means to disagree and repudiate means to reject. Now look at the first blank. The first blank is referring to something all great chess players know. The clue tells us that they know stubbornness will lead to mistakes that will force a player to capitulate to the prevailing strategy of their opponent. As you can see, we needed to solve for the second blank first, as we would not have known what stubbornness would lead to without doing so. Recycle the word stubbornness as your word for the blank. Obdurate is the only word that works for the first blank. Finicky means to be overly particular and vituperative means to be combative.

3. Corruptibility, venal, and redundancy

The first two blanks are related, but there isn't a strong clue for either one in the first part, so let's start with the third blank. Since the motif is tiresome, the third blank must mean something close to "repetitive." Redundancy matches this. At the end of the paragraph, each character is bribed ... into giving up ... beliefs. So the first two blanks must mean "bribable." Corruptibility in the first blank and venal in the second both match this.

4. Illegal and unabashedly

For the first blank, the clues "pirating software" and "downloading software from unapproved sources" describe unauthorized activities, and illegal is the best ıt. Uncommon and difficult are incorrect because the sentence says that "many people continue to do so." If people are doing something despite its illegality and "almost as if they were unaware that such acts amount to theft" you could describe them as acting brashly. Unabashedly is the best fit.

5. Insolvent

The phrase "squandered his life's savings on unpotable business ventures" tells you that the entrepreneur had no money left. The blank needs a word that means broke. Former and unlikely are tempting choices, but they don't match broke. Eliminate them. Eccentric also doesn't match, while perturbed only describes the entrepreneur's possible feelings. Insolvent agrees with the clue, so keep it.

6. Eschew obfuscation, recondite, and limpid

The key clue is that the teachers urge students to "use clear, simple language." The trigger instead indicates that the phrase that goes into the blank will present an alternative to using clear, simple language, while the and indicates that the phrase will nevertheless agree with the clue. Something like "avoid difficult language" would be best: difficult language is the alternative to clear, simple language, but the two phrases still agree because the difficult language is something to avoid. Thus, eschew obfuscation is best: Eschew means avoid, while obfuscation means the act of hiding the meaning of something. Exscind obloquy means to cut out critical language, while evince ossification means to show excessive rigidity, neither of which is appropriate here. The second blank needs a word that means difficult or obscure because teachers call into question the use of difficult vocabulary; recondite means obscure and hard to understand. Recreant means cowardly; redolent means fragrant. The final blank requires a word like clear because that is the type of language that "conveys one's meaning so much more effectively." Limpid means easily understood, and so is correct.

7. A and C

Answer choice (A) is supported because the passage says that myelin protects the brain's circuitry. Answer choice (C) is supported by the fact that "as humans mature" increasing levels of myelin need to be produced. While the passage suggests that a lack of myelin leaves the brain vulnerable, that doesn't mean that increasing the levels of myelin will reverse damage.

8. B

In the passage, byzantine refers to the "circuitry inside our nervous systems." Previously, the circuitry is described as growing more complex, so you need to find a word with a similar meaning. Answer choice (A) is an alternate meaning for byzantine, but is not supported by the passage. Answer choices (C), (D), and (E) do not have meanings similar to complex.

9. D

The argument concludes that large universities should utilize work-study students rather than administrative assistants. The premise is that a similar strategy realizes a cost savings at small colleges. This is an argument by analogy. Hence, the argument assumes that there are similar conditions at small colleges and at large universities. Choice (D) says that students at universities are just as qualified to take over the administrative roles as they are in small colleges. In other words, the administrative jobs at universities are not appreciably different than those at colleges. For choice (A), whether the practice would be of greater benefit to the small colleges is out of scope. For choice (B), whether large universities usually depend on small colleges for ideas is out of scope. For choice (C), the issue of nonwork-study students is out of scope. For choice (E), whether anyone has an easier ride than anyone else is out of scope.

10. A

The first paragraph acts as an introduction to the rest of the passage. The author notes that in the nineteenth century "investments became increasingly speculative." In the last paragraph, the author explains that due to fluctuatin interest rates, the consol was popular with speculative investors. There is no support in the passage for (B), (C), or (D). Although the first paragraph provides a historical framework, as suggested in answer choice (E), it does not provide a way "by which the nature of the nineteenth-century investor" could be understood.

11. To address the problem, the British government instituted a sinking fund, using tax revenue to buy back the bonds in the open market. The second paragraph has five sentences so this question has five answer choices. The third sentence begins, "To address the problem...." This is a clear indication that the sentence describes a solution to a problem. The correct answer is the third sentence.

12. Rarefied and meager

What sort of atmosphere would make Mars the only planet "whose surface details can be discerned from Earth?" You need a word that means transparent or thin for the blank. Viscous takes you in the wrong direction, so toss it. The next choice, ossified, makes no sense; toss that one, too. In contrast, rarefied works well, so hang onto it. Meanwhile, a copious atmosphere would definitely not be easy to see through, so cross out that choice. Meager fits nicely and agrees with rarefied, making those two the best answers.

13. Adversity and tribulation

The clue is "Using the hardships of the Joad family as a model." Recycle hardships, and use POE. Does reticence mean hardships? No; cross it out. Adversity works, so leave it. Do the same for the remaining choices. Only tribulation agrees with hardships, so that's the other correct answer.

14. A venerable and an august The blank is a description of the pyramid. The clue is "imposing structure" because this is the only other description of the pyramid. Venerable and august are the only words that match imposing.

15. Noisome and mephitic

The word that fills the blank must describe "the stench of the livestock," which is so malodorous that it drives the newcomers back to the city; it must mean something like, well, stinky! Both noisome and mephitic are appropriate choices. The other words don't work; if you were tempted by olfactory, realize that it simply means "related to the sense of smell" and does not actually describe a particular scent.

16. B

Answer choice (B) correctly sums up the purpose of the passage: It explores the significance—the creation of a military aristocracy and chivalric culture—of a technological innovation—the stirrup. Choice (A) is incorrect because nothing in the passage suggests that this discussion has a basis in recent discovery. Answer choice (C) is too broad for the limited subject matter discussed. Choice (D) is too extreme. Answer choice (E) is incorrect because the physics, while important in connecting the stirrup to its social effects, isn't really the point of the passage— and, in any event, the physics relates to cavalry, not artillery.

17. E

Answer choice (E) is supported by the passage because the sixth sentence suggests that the development of the barbed lance serves as an "unusually clear" marker. Choice (A) is incorrect because no additional subjects for research are brought up in the passage. Choices (B) and (C) require comparisons beyond the scope of the information in the passage: No other technology, ancient or medieval, was discussed. Answer choice (D) however , is an extreme overstatement: Although the stirrup increased the military value of the horse, nowhere is it suggested that it had previously been considered militarily insignificant.

18. "Stirrups unify lance, rider, and horse into a force capable of unprecedented violence."

In this sentence, the author says that stirrups improve the ability of a lance and rider. This is an improvement on the issues discussed earlier when the author states that a "lance couched under the rider's arm, unifying the force of rider and weapon, would throw its wielder backwards off the horse at impact."

19. D

Choice (D) describes the organization of the passage. Answer choice (A) can be eliminated because the traditional definition is never amended. Answer choice (B) can be eliminated because the authorities do not support the traditional theory. Answer choice (C) can be eliminated because no new version is proposed. Answer choice (E) can be eliminated because the "implications of the experiment" are not rejected.

20. A and B

The author's dismissal of the traditional definition of randomness rests upon the premises that the results of the same probabilistic mechanism will all have the same likelihood of occurring, and, as such, should be considered equally probable. The passage never mentions how the results of divergent probabilistic mechanisms relate to each other, so eliminate choice (C).

Made in the USA
Monee, IL
14 May 2020